TONIC *for* GREAT LIFE

ForeWord Reviews

Clarion Review

Tonic for Great Life: Are You Ready for the Leap?

Kiran Kurwade

PartridgeIndia

978-1-4828-1020-2

Four Stars (out of Five)

"This intriguing book is steeped in a life philosophy that builds up the individual and **_encourages self-awareness._**

The easiest way to describe Tonic for Great Life, an intriguing and somewhat puzzling book, is to call it an exercise in either spiritual philosophy or philosophical spirituality. The juxtaposition of words is quite intentional, since word reversal, word rhyme, word analysis, and word play are all part of the author's unusual writing style.

The book is steeped in a life philosophy that builds up the individual, encourages self-awareness, promotes lifelong learning, celebrates uniqueness, and appreciates the wholeness of intellect, emotion, body, and spirit. With its strong spiritual foundation, this is a work that could very well make one think about the fundamental meaning of life. That is essentially what author Kiran Kurwade means by "tonic"; he writes, "Tonic for the soul or transforming your Good Life to Great Life is knowing the truth in totality, which includes your unique strengths (Great Gifts) and utilizing them in Great Spirit."

Kurwade is skilled at expressing himself in language that is poetic and enticing. In fact, he uses and analyzes words in a unique way.

The following are a few of the phrases he employs in his book: "The moment you conquer your inner rival is the moment of self-revival"; "God is nowhere or God is now here"; "Every Stone can be a Milestone"; "Invisible doesn't mean not visible but in-visible (visible inside)"; and "Any Role without Goal is like a Body without Soul." At the close of each chapter, Kurwade includes "Good Morning Tonic," a collection of sayings such as the ones above, followed by a space for the reader to write his or her own tonic. These tonics are then reprised at the end of the book so the reader has a complete collection of them, all in one place.

Another intriguing element of the text is Kurwade's excellent use of black-and-white photography. Each high-quality photograph seems perfectly matched to one of the author's philosophical tonics. In addition, the interior pages are well-designed and the fanciful cover image is stunning.

So, for the reader who is looking to explore his or her inner self, gain spiritual enlightenment, and be entertained by a writer who has a novel way of expressing himself, Tonic for Great Life is a good choice."

"Kiran Kurwade has written a gem to be treasured in the world of self-improvement literature."—GoodbooksToday.com Reviews

Written by experienced behavioral coach Kiran Kurwade, Tonic for Great Life: Are You Ready for the Leap? is a self-help book imbibed with insightful words of wisdom, discovered by Kiran Kurwade himself while on his pursuit for spiritual enlightenment and peace. Tonic for Great Life is divided into several chapters, aimed at developing your mindset, intelligence, relationships and leadership skills. Tonic for Great Life is geared towards helping develop corporate leaders, or improving the lifestyle and skills of existing corporate leaders. A refreshing read in a fast-paced, competitive world, Tonic for Great Life offers practical, simple solutions to achieving a work-life balance and a fulfilling career. It cleanses the mind in a cluttered world of the many demands of the human body and soul. Besides offering great advice, Tonic for Great Life is written from the heart in full honesty and humility—it reaches out to the reader in a wholehearted attempt to improve their lives. A sprinkling of inspiring quotes and pictures adorn the book, adding an elegant touch to an already beautiful piece of work. Meaningful real-life anecdotes are used to convey important messages. For the reader's convenience, there is a summary page of major takeaways and inspiring quotes at the end of the book.

Having 18 years of work experience, several training workshops and 5000 workshop attendees under his belt, Kiran Kurwade is well-qualified to write Tonic For Great Life. He has instilled his passion for helping others into this delightful read. Tonic for Great Life is truly inspiring. Reading this book would be akin to attending one of his training workshops in person, but at a very economical price. Kiran Kurwade has written a gem to be treasured in the world of self-improvement literature. Read Tonic for Great Life to enhance your relationships with your family, friends and co-workers, as well as to achieve a fulfilling work-life balance while achieving personal growth and scaling the corporate ladder.

TONIC *for* GREAT LIFE

Are you ready for the leap?
A Humble, Holistic & Harmonious Leap . . .

KIRAN KURWADE

PARTRIDGE
A Penguin Random House Company

To order additional copies of this book, contact
Partridge India
000 800 10062 62
www.partridgepublishing.com/india
orders.india@partridgepublishing.com

CONTENTS

I dedicate *"Tonic for Great Life"* to every fellow traveller of Truth, aspiring and inspiring a Conscious & Compassionate Life

Can we honestly meditate on the question **"Are we God fearing or God nearing people?"** 'Tonic for Great Life' is for those who believe (be & live) in Love, and Love has no fear hence it is being God nearing because Love is God.

Medicine, Meditation and Motivation is same, which can be at times bitter but brings out the better in us.

This book is like a seed (nuggets) and not a readymade flower or fruit. When the seeker sows the seed, nurtures with his own way and gets the fruit then he rejoices his ownership. *Until we accomplish such enlightenment i.e. the flowering, we live as restless souls.*

Raah wahi jisme apni rooh se bhi riha ho jaye raahi

I am just a kid who has taken few baby steps . . .

With gratitude—Kiran Kurwade

My perception of Soul is Spirit of Universal Love, I would prefer to take spirit as a synergizing attitude (energy) and not to dwell much in esoteric concept.

Materialistic has every luxury but no peace and Spiritualist has peace but struggles to pay money of school fees for his children. Great Life is not living in either extremes, it is all about *holistic, healthy & happy* growth.

A Great Leap is from One to Oneness.

By Kiran Kurwade

FOREWORD

Chaos, crime, confusion, cut throatism and corruption are all synonymous with the prevailing society scenario. Resultant; frustration, anguish, anxiety, hatred, fear and materialism has made the present generation restless, reckless, confused, intolerant and self-centered. This book 'Tonic for Great Life', therefore, could not have come at a more appropriate time than this.

The author, through this book, discusses with the reader, how even today, a positive, purposeful and peaceful life is possible, if full potential of a human being is exploited by synergy of his mind, heart, soul and body. He has very beautifully articulated the connect between truth, love, efficiency and sharing in the development of a wholesome personality as well as the chain that links ability to 'Conceive' with the ability to 'Achieve', through the rungs of 'Devotion' & 'Divinity'.

The issue of 'Self" being a part of 'We' and responsibilities of great professionals towards the society have been very nicely discussed and the supremacy of the 'Deeds' over the 'Persona' has been very aptly brought out. The author rightly does not subscribe to the view that one can only take a horse to the pond but cannot make it drink water. He rightly brings out that such an attitude is only indicative of the inability of the handler rather than the stubbornness of the animal.

In my view, the book eminently succeeds in discussing with the reader, the key to leading a harmonious, holistic & happy life. To the young generation of today, it will certainly provide the much needed 'TONIC' to push out negativity from their minds and life style.

I congratulate Kiran for his brilliant work. It gives me immense happiness to endorse this book that, reflects the genius in this young man.

Maj Gen (Retd) SP Kapoor, VSM
Ex GOC HQ ATNKK&G Area.
EX Member, State Consumer Commission, UT, Chandigarh

VIEWS AND REVIEWS

Kiran has done a phenomenal job in putting together in this book, the wisdom and insights he has gathered first hand through his several years of single minded pursuit of spiritual development. Anyone who wants to live a life that is less stressful and more meaningful, will benefit from this work. **Rajiv R. Gupta, CEO, EGE Global Education and alumnus of Harvard Business School**

A masterpiece of self-introspection process, it will help readers to know Who am I? This can bring sea change in one's personal and professional life by adopting practical techniques. **Shekhar Jyoti, COO, Videocon Ind. Ltd.**

*I met Kiran at Riyadh in 2012. It was a great experience, I'll never forget the course delivered by him which I glimpsed in this book.—***Nasser Al Ghilan, Saudi Airlines Customer Services Trainer, Riyadh, KSA.**

"Tonic for Great Life is an articulate and highly readable synthesis of current thinking on change and framework to apply in real life situations. I recommend it for all leaders and development professionals." **G. Abbas Wafa, Advisor, Justice Sector Support Program Kabul, Afghanistan**

Kiran has done a fabulous job of understanding our collective consciousness. The book inspires us to look within and takes us through a humble journey filled with profound anecdotes. In a world where dealing with stress has become a platitude, "Tonic for Great life" shines as a beacon for those who wish to realize their true potential. **S. Krithivasan, GM, Hotel Ambassador Pallava, Chennai**

A must read for management students. **Raman Preet, Executive Director, Pune Institute of Business Management**

Kiran has chosen to write simply because he is endowed with total self-belief and has the fortitude to live it. I consider it as a big leap for the world of Management, particularly in the Indian context. Others too will gain by and by. **Brig Vivek Sohal, Sena Medal (Retd)**

I know Kiran from school days. The change I have seen in him over the last few years has been truly remarkable, and I think this book is just an attempt to share his belief in life and self with all of us. It doesn't matter whether the reader is a student, professional, sportsman or just a layman—there is something in it for each one of us. **Sanjeev Moghe, Sr Vice President in a leading multi-national bank. An alumnus—IIT Bombay and IIM Calcutta. Author's schoolmate**

AT THE FEET OF MOTHER

One day a busy manager during his weekly off takes his old mother for shopping along with the family. While the wife and children were shopping, the man gets to spend some time with his mother. The Mother insists to go to a place where she used to come with him many years ago when he was a small boy. The mother and son then go to visit the nostalgic place, where many birds come and people feed them grains.

They sit for some time and the mother questions the son about a bird, "Which bird is this? Son replies "Wild pigeon" Mother asks again and son gives the same reply, mother repeats the question and this time son gets angry and says, "I told you, its wild pigeon, don't you understand?" Mother replies with a heavy voice and moistened eyes, "Son, when you were young, you had asked this question at this place many times and every time I had kissed your forehead and replied lovingly feeling nothing but love for you . . ." (Source: Unknown)

If at all the world exists amidst so much of chaos . . . it's only because of loving beings and owing to true love instilled, illuminated & inspired by a mother.

Thank you Mother!
Kiran Kurwade

PREFACE

What is a TONIC for Great Life? Yes, it is a Quest to get the Best. A Quest for the restless souls, it enthuses, educates and empowers to take a Great Leap!

There is hardly any human being in the world who does NOT wish to:

- Be Loved and Love
- Live as much as possible or if possible Live forever
- Grow infinitely (e.g. businessmen want to scale up as much as possible)

There is **_something_** in us that is pure Love, Eternal & Infinite. Knowing and living such "Truth" is a Tonic for Great Life. **_Until we accomplish enlightenment of life, we live as restless souls._**

Are you ready for the Great Leap? **_Great Leap is of one to oneness, known to unknown, finite to infinite, mortal to immortal._** Of a drop to ocean and every drop has a ripple effect. Example, when a great freedom fighter dies while fighting for the great cause he becomes an inspiration for infinite beings, stays in their hearts as true love forever and thus becomes eternal. Unless we die to the past we cannot fly for the future. It's a transcendence of Me to We. The 'We' is all pervading and encompassing i.e. the entire universe.

How my current life is different from great life? A good life may help you to be good as an individual person, but can keep you divided, thus making you feel stressed; whereas great life helps you to realize the "Truth" that you are a part of love, which is eternal and infinite making you an integral part of the Universe and keeping you integrated and blissful.

Am I happy with my current life? Most of us today are living a good life because of the developed economy, and people have higher disposable incomes. We witnessed a huge development in technology, internet, education, media, transportation etc. However, we have realized living a good life is not blissful rather it is more stressful. Under such duress, how can we enjoy life in its truest sense? In a mad race of being good, we have turned ourselves into 'goods' (things, in a material sense). It is not that such people do not want to contribute towards society, it is that they crave to be labelled as 'good,' a hero, and claim their work to be the only good possible. Thus, it is of little wonder, at backstage they end up doing many bad things.

Some good people aspire to move from good to great. There has to be something that enables us to move from a good life to a great life.

What are the barriers when moving from good life to a great life? We are too lazy or busy to know the way out and then walk towards it. Following can be the few reasons:

- **Illusion is 'ill Vision,'**—when our vision becomes ill, it creates an illusion. However we remain unaware of this illusion, and turn into **Happy Slaves.**
- We live in an era of information, an age of speed and a world of instant gratification. Instant Coffee and Instant Break-ups, have become the flavour of the day. We always seem to be in a big hurry, missing out the great things of life.
- Unfortunately, most of us use our intelligence in a way akin to digging a well every now and then to quench our thirst and often keep pouring water in a vessel that has no base.
- Many boast that they have adequate knowledge but most of them fail to achieve their goals, and even if they achieve are unable to enjoy it.
- If the person is not action oriented and result oriented, then there is no difference between him and his photograph hanging on a wall. Action reflects our Vision.

What has to be done? Some **TONIC is required**, isn't it? **If we take tonic to revive our sick body then we should also take tonic to** revive our soul. Tonic for the soul or transforming your Good Life to Great Life is knowing the truth in totality, which includes your unique strengths (Great Gifts) and utilizing them in Great Spirit. First, one must Trust himself/herself to know and live the Truth.

Know your Unique Strength/Great Gift: Knowing one's own weaknesses is good, but to focus on the strengths is even better. **Everybody is UNIQUE** and possesses some unique strength . . . be it an individual, a brand, an organization or a nation. We must know our strengths, work on it consistently and emerge strong, and only then the Higher Strength will naturally merge in us. Because, as like attracts like . . . . so strong attracts strong.

'B' Positive may not be everyone's blood group, but from womb to tomb it runs in all of us and changes us from me to we, idle to ideal, and good to great!

What is the significance of Unique Strength/Great Gift? **Let us look at an analogy: a tiny stem of a tree, which attaches the fruit to a branch**.

It seemingly looks tiny and weak, but holds the much bigger fruit. The stem represents people who derive all the resources, processes, and knowledge from the Tree. Tree represents the society or an organization, and the Fruit can be the common people around us or customers. The 'stem' functions as GOD—Generator, Operator & Destroyer. The fruit is born on the stem, which supplies all nutrients, holds the fruit and one day breaks away when the fruit is ready and ripe. Breaking away is like giving freedom when it is ready. When a ripe fruit falls down, it's seeds spread all over, creating new trees. The destruction is pseudo-destruction, it is transformation, or we can say continuous creation or generation.

Believe in your Strengths, and Build your Strengths so that nothing will Beat you.

How to move from Good life to Great Life? God has created food for all birds, but He does not throw it in their nests, even if it is the best nest. The food must necessarily to be earned through hard labour.

Today's world is highly competitive, hence to live a Great Life one must possess certain basic competencies.

Through the analogy of "Role of a tiny Stem of Tree" we have realized we must accept our existential reality, and it will *enthuse, enable and empower* us to move from good to great. *Wherever we are, that forms to be the entry point.* Here it must be noted that unique strength varies from person to person, but eventually leads to a common or universal strength that is present in all sentient beings. It is the common denominator, so to be one with that strength is the actual transcendence of Good to Great life.

Journey of Good life to Great life is an amalgamation of mind (Good life) and soul (Great life). Hence, it is essential to understand it in totality. This book is an honest attempt to enable you to know your unique strengths/great gifts and utilize it to the fullest potential. We will co-explore in the chapters on how to be in the present, how to create a great self, how to know and actualize your great gift, why learning discipline is required, what is great intelligence, how to arrive a great solution, what are great relationships and responsibility of being a great professional, leader and change maker. I feel, the greatest miracle is to be compassionate towards all at all times. Conscious & Compassionate living is my tonic.

In many chapters of this book, you will come across the word TONIC, which means Truth or Totality. It is the Quest to get the Best.

Also, every chapter will have '*Good Morning Tonic*' in the form of insights, relevant to the subject as conceived by Kiran Kurwade, are exclusively mentioned towards the end of book.

All the Best!
With gratitude,
Kiran Kurwade

ACKNOWLEDGEMENT

I gratefully acknowledge the great insights received over the years from my school teachers, grandparents, parents, In-laws, family, friends, bosses that I lived and worked with, and every being (living or non-living), the time and places wherein I received inspiration for living a *positive, purposeful and practical life* . . .

When I was five, I used to listen to *Ramayana, Mahabharatha and Dhammapada* from my great grandmother. As a child, I preferred spending time alone and contemplating on life. At a very young age, teachings of Buddha and the word "Enlightenment" had mesmerizing effects on me, and soon I had a strong feeling that if at all I have to accomplish anything then it is not becoming rich in a material sense, but living a conscious and compassionate life.

In 1995, I read few books written by Osho given by my friend Santosh Dakhe and my perspective towards life changed dramatically. It was a kind of self-validation of my understanding as a child. Some of the stories are sourced from Osho's discourses that I often listen to meditatively. I thank Eknath Kadam for teaching me meditations.

I spent a few years visiting the Osho Commune Pune regularly from 1998 to 2004, and attended few meditation camps. Besides this, I did Vipassana at Igatpuri, read and watched videos of Jiddu Krishnamurti, and I am highly touched by his teachings too. Since 2005, I have been reading and watching many videos of Scientology & Dianetics, it is playing a crucial role in my life and helping me to function effectively as a Soft Skills trainer. During my early years of corporate life, I received practical lessons of management from Mr. S. Krithivasan, the then GM of a five star hotel. The principles learned from him formed to be the stepping-stones in my professional life.

My life received the correct direction when I met Mr. Rajeev Bhaskar Sahi in 2004 at Mumbai, the then President of one of the biggest Indian conglomerate in the world. I had joined there as a trainer. In the very first interaction with him, my inner voice said, *"Kiran, this is the guru . . . your guru."* That was a turning point of my life as a trainer and as a person, and sitting through his sessions turned out to be one of the greatest blessings in my life. My ex-boss Mr. Rajiv Gupta, author of *'Spirituality Demystified'* has also inspired me greatly. I am fortunate to receive personal tips on my training and writing skills from Late Shri Rooshikumar Pandya, a renowned international behavioural coach and a great scholar. I am grateful to Mr. Shekhar Jyoti, a COO with one of the fastest growing corporate companies in India, and I am still learning the practicalities of corporate life from him. I am grateful to all my friends especially Mr. Nasser Al Ghilan from Saudi Arabia for teaching me about Islam. It is a great learning experience of my life.

At family front; to name a few . . . I would like to express my gratitude for my grandparents Yadavrao and Shakuntala, for sowing seeds of compassion in me. My mother Saraswati for breathing a wonderful life in me, my father Limbaji, a retired army officer for instilling in me a sense of Self-Discipline, my father-in-law Dr. B.P. Engade for having faith in me always, my wife Dr. Kranti for holding my hand at every turn of life and my son Maitreya, my great gift from Almighty, and watching him smiling is a great joy of my life. I thank Prabhanjan Mahatole for giving me an entrepreneurial platform iWin.

I am grateful to Maj General S K Kapoor, Brig Vivek Sohal and Mr. Shekhar Jyoti for being an inspiration for all at Kurwade family.

The origin of the book is from my daily updates on Facebook and the e-mailers I used to mail to one of the corporate companies as motivational stuff. It was from here that a thought occurred to me in 2004, when I realized that through a book I can enable people to think and enquire about life from a more holistic and honest perspective.

I thank Radley Machado for sharing some of the images photographed by him.

With gratitude—Kiran Kurwade

Nature of Matter is to Revolve and of non-Matter is to Evolve.

By Kiran Kurwade

NOTHING DIES HERE

Flowing in wind,
Memoirs unwind,
That once I was wind!

Lit up in fire,
Memoirs respire,
That once I was fire!

Grounded in Earth,
Memoirs take birth,
That once I was Earth!

Floating in water,
Memoirs shatter,
That once I was water!

Flying in the sky,
Memoirs fly,
That once I was sky!

Memoirs explode feeling,
Feeling implode eternal Being,
Being is no-thing so it is everything!

No person is new, I feel I met him before,
No place is new, I feel I been here before,
This presence and consciousness is ever fresh as before!

Me, You, They . . . is just One,
Sometimes rise sometime fall,
Like waves of same ocean!

But who is this Knower?
Knower has to be separate from the Known,
So, I am just pristine and eternal Watcher!

But Watcher indicates some Doing,
And this Doing is also Watched,
So, I am just Being!

Knower and Known is one here,
Transforms but Indestructible,
So Nothing Dies Here!

Love & Light
Kiran Kurwade

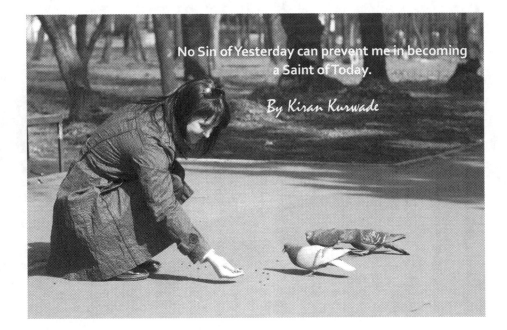

No Sin of Yesterday can prevent me in becoming a Saint of Today.

By Kiran Kurwade

1

Tonic for Now & Here

**Live this moment as if it is Last because it will never Last.
Live the Best, Leave the Rest!**

Being in the 'Now' is foremost; therefore, it is the first chapter of the book. As we know there is nothing that has not gone through the Now, so this sets up the right tone to derive the best possible insights for a greater life. Being in the Now is a prelude to rest of the book. If I can feel the leaf, I can rest in the forest.

Once a father and his young son from a poor family, happened to visit a seashore during sunrise. The son said to his father, "*Father, it is such a beautiful scene, Alas! if we had a camera, we could have taken a lovely picture of the sunrise.*" Father replied, "*Son, watch the scene with your soul; click the picture with your eyes and preserve it in your heart . . . you will remember it forever.*"

How much of our life do we remember? We may not remember everything, but we cannot forget our happiest moments and our saddest moments. How can we forget our first day of school, the first kiss, first day of college, first day of job, first night of marriage, first public presentation? Neither can we forget the moment when somebody may have forced us to do something at a gunpoint, nor the day we were awarded publicly for some outstanding achievement.

Why do we remember such incidences, events or accidents? This is because during such moments there is no movement of our thoughts, it is 100% in the 'Now'. During such moments, our **consciousness** is at its peak, and we have a choice of *flight or fight*. We either become **unconscious** in case of *'flight'* succumbing to the situation or the accident (it gets recorded in our **sub-conscious** and often we are driven by it without we knowing it clearly), OR we become **super-conscious** in case of *'fight'* choosing to be in the 'Now,' at any cost until the last moment.

Being in Now enables you to minimize accidents and maximize events. Living in Now is a master key to access the sub-conscious, it is being alive, or else it is living mechanical.

We will explore 'Now' holistically but before this let us explore what we know of Time.

What is Time? Can we say 'Time' is the space between two happenings? Time is broadly divided into Chronological Time and Psychological Time. Chronological Time is linear, i.e. if today is 21st June 2013, and then tomorrow will be 22nd June, so on and so forth. Time is irreversible. Chronological Time is beyond our control, so there are no questions of managing it. On the other hand, Psychological Time is non-linear, i.e. we live and re-live the moments, as we desire. When we are young, we tend to live in the future, dreaming of the best possible profession, house, name, fame etc. When we grow old, we live in the past, remembering how good were the days of our childhood, often referring them as the 'golden days.'

Therefore, psychologically, time is relative, i.e. when we are with our beloved then we fall short of time, and when we are in unbearable pain, then time moves slowly. Psychological Time is a personal perspective. So the question is **can we end the Psychological Time? Yes, it can be done, because i**t is dependent on our likes and dislikes, comforts and discomforts i.e. one one's **Self**. Hence, psychological time can be controlled and conquered. We shall know in detail about 'Self,' in one of our chapters *'Tonic for Great Self.'* The immediate response would be an art of living within Now.

If we can live in Now, then we can end the psychological time.

Do we manage Time or does Time manage us?

Time—Change—Stress, are interlinked because time is the space between two events (changes), everything is changing and goals are time lined.

Most of the reviews on Time Management deal with management science. We attend the training programs, read certain books, and feel good for some time, then fall back to our old habits because we do not explore it in totality.

Time has to be explored from all possible dimensions of life, like **psychological**, **spiritual** and **scientific** dimensions, along with management studies. Science has a relevant formula, Speed=Distance/Time. So, Time = Distance/Speed. Psychologically, time is felt as short and long, as we have already seen. Spiritually, Time =Now. Everything is contained within Now. Thus, the major task is to align all the aforementioned dimensions.

As for example, when we do anything that we truly love then our speed automatically becomes very high, and we find ourselves in the Now. Now is Truth. We can fake everything, but how can we fake the very 'present' i.e. Now?

What is Now? Now which we also refer to as the Present time can be for just a split second or may be for a very long time. Conventionally, it is always relative in nature. You may say, *"The first word on this page I read is past, it is no more Now."* Well, it is a vicious circle to find out which is the exact 'present' moment, hence miserable to live, because we will always remain confused, being highly analytical with good IQ. At times too much analysis becomes a mental paralysis.

If you are aware of your past then you are in the present. It is easy. If we are present in the Present then we will be able to see clearly the past, present and future all together. It is said past is finite and future infinite because past is known and future is unknown. I feel the known is finite; either it is past or future, and unknown is infinite. In the context of time, there is no beginning and no end, while past and future both are infinite. 'Now' is actually transcendence of time and it's second and third dimension of linear and non-linear functions respectively. It is a leap from sequence to simultaneity and beyond. Hence, it is a great leap from time to timeless.

Generally we tend to become so immersed in an interesting activity that we turn a blind eye, as regards what is going on around us that may adversely affect our fast paced and multi-tasked life, and the more we bind, the more blinder we become. Another grim reality of today's generation is struggling to be 'attentive' at a given time while doing a given assignment, thus leaving many projects undone. We are unable to give quality time to our families or jobs. When we are with our families, we think of our jobs and while at work, think of our families. Attention Deficit Disorder exists in such a lifestyle. So what do we do now?

The moment you conquer your inner rival is the moment of self-revival.

By Kiran Kurwade

Take a Great Leap, Now & Here: Hence, practicing Self Awareness is a tonic. Self-Awareness has such an immense effect that it helps to live holistically in the Now. Self-Awareness is a quality of being aware that you are aware. You can refer to an insightful story mentioned in the next chapter "Tonic for great Learner" under the topic, 'Are you aware that you are aware?'

It is not only about being short-termed or long-termed in nature, one has to be short termed (microscopic) enough to beat the present challenges and long termed (macroscopic) enough to meet all future challenge.

We have a lot of literature on how to live in the Now, as this topic always attracted many philosophers and spiritualists in the past.

"Silent" and "Listen" are spelled with the same letters.

Approach: It is a common saying "Don't see how many moments constitute life but see how much life exists in each moment."

Meditation, feeling and controlling your own breath, or sensing whatever is going on around, would bring you to the present moment. Unwinding yourself with your hobby is a wonderful way to remain in the Now. What is your own style? Fasting (abstaining from food) is a common practice, which enables to live in Now and unleash our spiritual power. In this logic-oriented world, often, illogical things can be remembered easily. As for example if I have a habit of uttering certain words when I face a problem or get upset, I will promise to self that today I am not going to utter this word. It is a kind of fasting, a 'verbal' fasting. It will help me to be self-aware, alert and watchful. If I am right-handed person and eat food with my right hand, then one day in a week I will not use the right hand but work with my left hand. There could be any such activity that could act as a self-reminder, which would enable us to live in the Present. Living in Now is akin to cleaning the dust accumulated in our minds and access the sub-conscious.

Unless I die to the past, I cannot fly for the future.

Aids: Keeping in mind the multiple dimensions of time and our hectic schedules, we have to find out the most suitable ways of managing time i.e. managing Self. The foremost is mastering an art of living within Now. Nevertheless, knowing few of the widely accepted and practiced concepts can help you in your daily life, such as, Important & Urgent Matrix, Urgency Index, 3Ps—Planning, Prioritization & Procrastination and Prioritization Model. We will receive Tips & Techniques like Diary Management, Checklists, Planners, Effective utilization of Technology and Resources, Designing Robust Systems and Standard Processes and People Management Skills.

A very interesting point in this context is Procrastination. Why do we procrastinate? The reason can be derived from our habits. It is mostly the habits that drive us; therefore, we are called as habitats. We tend to do the things, which we are not supposed to do. Urgency Index also bottles down to habits. Old habits die hard, but can be conquered, and the tonic is to study the multiple dimensions viz. spiritual, psychological and scientific dimensions

Let us ask ourselves the following three questions;

- **Who is the most important person?**
- **Which is the most important time?**
- **What is the most important thing to do?**

The most important person is the person you are dealing with in the Now, the most important thing to do is to give your 100% attention, hence the most important time is Now. This is true justice. All changes take place within Now.

Let's take the case of a salesperson, unless he or she is 100% in the Now, he/she cannot effectively attend to customers, cannot know what the customer really wants, hence cannot provide the best product or service.

I feel, **experience** is synonymous to **expiry**; it has 'ex' in it, which means past. Experience is good, but if we are conditioned to it, then we are living in past. If we do not face the present then we will miss the new moments, since life is continuum. Every moment is new and in this, we see everything new. Being in Now is being soulful. The great news is that everything looks new when we see it with our souls. Unfortunately, at last minute, we realize its power. Who knows better the value of hair than a bald man? Only when things are taken away from us, do we realize its importance. It can be a job, beloved or life itself. The happy memories make us feel strong and sad memories make us feel weak; psychologically, spiritually and physically.

The one who is present 100% in the present can present the best present.

By Kiran Kurwade

Good Morning Tonic

- Jisne 'aaj' ko jeeta, usne har 'taj' ko jeeta
- The great news is that things look New when we see it through the Soul.
- No Sin of yesterday can prevent me from becoming a Saint today.
- Wisdom lies in integrating all the dimensions and transcending from time to timelessness. If I want to RELIEVE myself then I've to RE-LIVE the unlived moments more consciously and compassionately.
- Space & Time is one, No Space, No Time.
- Infinite Space, Infinite Time.
- Let us widen our vision to see the infinite space and that is being truly in Now.
- The more I Sleep, the more I Slip

Space to write your own tonic

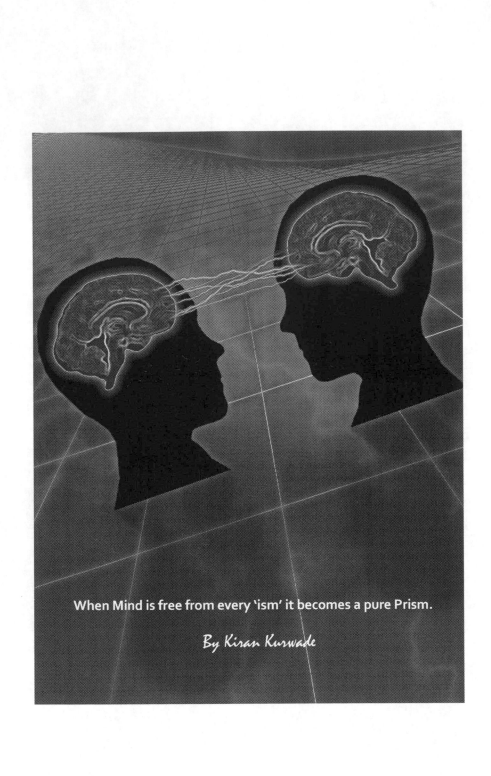

When Mind is free from every 'ism' it becomes a pure Prism.

By Kiran Kurwade

2

Tonic for Great Learner

Who is a great Learning Aspirant? What qualities he should possess? What is the biggest barrier in Learning? Let us co-explore through few stories and analogies . . .

Learn, UNLEARN and Relearn: This incidence dates back to the period where there was no electricity in India. One night a blind man was invited for dinner to his friend's house. After dinner when the blind man was about to leave, his friend gives him a lantern. The blind man said, "*I do not need a lantern, darkness or light is all the same to me.*" His friend replied, "*I know you do not need a lantern to find your way but if you don't have one, someone else on the road may accidently run into you. So you must take it.*"

The blind man took it and started walking with the lantern. After some time, he started walking very carelessly. He was nearly knocked over by a stranger on a bicycle. The stranger was angry and warned him to walk carefully. However, the blind man arrogantly said, "*Are you blind, can't you see this lantern?*" The stranger said, "*Your lantern has no light, be careful brother*". The night was windy and the lantern had blown off.

Borrowed knowledge unless, experienced by one self is dangerous. Secondly, our own experiential knowledge of yesterday is history and may not be applicable today.

Another aspect, is that if we light a candle in our house and try to see the moon's brilliant light at the same time, it is not possible to view both together. As long as there is candle light, we will fail to see the moonlight inside our house. The moment candle light goes off the moonlight will become prominent. Many times our ego, i.e. little knowledge, becomes an obstacle in not understanding the bigger reality. The frog that remains inside a well remains deprived of the outside oceanic experience. For a learning aspirant, belief plays crucial role.

Are you Aware that you are Aware? Once three young friends approached a spiritual master to learn meditation and find the real meaning of life. The master gave a pigeon to each one of them and asked them to kill it, provided nobody knows about the killing. One boy took the pigeon far away in the forest where there were no human beings and killed the pigeon. The second one carried the pigeon to a cave, away from all animals and killed it. Third one went deeper into the cave, ensuring not even an insect is there, and tried killing it but realized he is watching, so he closed his eyes but again realized that even with eyes closed he is aware. Thus, he could not kill the pigeon. The master said to the first two boys that they are yet not ready to become his disciples. To the third boy he said, "You have got the right answer". **Self-awareness is the key to self-revelation, and in self-revelation there is the answer to life.**

There is similar insightful story of a man who goes to Zen Master to learn sword fight. The master instead of teaching him asked him to do trivial jobs like fetching water, cleaning, sweeping etc. and every now and then used to hit him suddenly with a stick. Many months passed and still the master continued assigning him non-related work and increased the frequency of hitting him without any reason. The disciple was tired and confused but did not give up, and continued following his master's instructions without questioning him. One day while he was asleep, the master raised a stick to hit him but the disciple sensed it this time, woke up and caught the stick. The Master said, *"Now you are ready, let us start learning sword fight"*

Thus, **Alertness is a basic requirement. Once you achieve total alertness, watchfulness, and self-awareness, then you can learn anything in totality.**

When we start hearing "Unable" as "Enable", we become an Able in true sense.

By Kiran Kurwade

Have a **FOCUS;** It can be **F**ind **O**ut **C**onsciously **U**ntil **S**ought **or F**ight **O**n **C**ontinuously **U**ntil **S**uccessful: An amazing quality of observation that is holistic, unbiased and sharp is vital. This is because when we are able to observe the thought, we are able to absorb it. Many people speak about Focus, it is good to have focus, but focus cannot be forced, it needs to be felicitated. Great interest preludes the focus.

Say, a famous movie star walks into a showroom to buy some apparels and she happens to be a favourite of the sales clerk. Invariably the sales clerk will be engrossed in attending to her needs, he will not forget the fragrance of her perfume, the colour of her attire, the way she walked and talked. Because she interests and excites him, hence the focus is automatic. The same sales clerk will not recall the details of ordinary customers.

When you learn in such a way, that you have to teach what you have learnt, then you learn more, remember more and teach more

Wake . . . Bake . . . Cake: If we deeply observe the process of baking a cake, we will get certain insights into emerging as a great learner.

Wake: When we closely observe the making of cake or bread or rotis, we will find that the first important step is kneading. Harder (heartier) the kneading, softer is the bread. I take it as waking up, because it's awakening up or loosening ourselves to get involved. The basic of life is **"Involve to Evolve"**. How important is waking up or kneading of self? How often and how well do we knead ourselves?

Kneading should avoid greed; else it will land up in mess. Kneading must be flexible so that we can take any form easily. Kneading is all-inclusive i.e. mixing well with all other ingredients. Do you gel well with your colleagues, customers and bosses? To fit rightly in any given role, flexibility is necessary. It is in fact enhancing your Learning Curve. How fast are you Learning and Implementing?

Bake: Just kneading is not sufficient. Baking is also very important. Baking is going through tough times, unbearable situations and facing challenging people. A diamond was once just a piece of coal, which went through high temperatures and pressure. Many times, we are tempted to take short cuts in life in order to avoid pain. Moreover, we may have many excuses but if the bake is a fake, then we will not get the delicious cake.

Cake: Great bake leads to great cake. Cake is being successful in delighting self and others. Great cakes are destined to be at the service of people often to mark as celebration of success. Are you in the making of a great Cake?

Please allow me to mention a quote by Richard Bach "Learning is finding out what we already know".

This insight enables me to understand that the question by itself is an answer but somehow the answer is forgotten. It is as if when we learn swimming we realize that we know it already. It is in our nature to float. This lightning echoes in my being, since I know that I exist in the present and much before that, as a fact. What is the gut feel? It reminds me of the making of my guts when I was in the womb of my mother and the knowledge I had assimilated by then. What is déjà vu or intuition? It reminds my Omni-presence that is beyond all physical elements.

When we are in water . . . do we not feel that we have been in the water before? and why do we get awestruck when we look at the sky? Don't we feel we are one with the sky? Never born, hence never died but existed as transient energy, which takes various forms, thoughts or dreams or bodies or avatars.

Visualize pure water, if we put a drop of blue colour to it, it becomes blue and if we then add a drop of red colour to it . . . it does not become pure red. Water has to become again nothing i.e. colourless in order to become hold a perfect or pure colour. It is a great art to remain persistently within the state of "nothingness" to experience 'anything' and 'everything'.

Attitude & Discipline: When we enumerate English alphabets i.e. A=1, B=2, C=3 . . . Z=26 and add up the corresponding numbers of A+T+T+I+T+U+D+E, it is equal to 100; similarly D+I+S+C+I+P+L+I+N+E is also = 100

Hence, discipline is as important as attitude. If we have the right attitude, but lack self-discipline, then it is futile. Discipline, a derivative of the word disciple, comes from within, one who is a disciple of life i.e. in continuous learning mode then he will be disciplined by own.

Learn from everybody and everything continuously: Focus plays a wonderful role in paying attention and grasping minute details. However, in today's multi-faceted world, high multi-tasking is a necessity, hence one must have broader observation capabilities and a power to absorb many things quickly, without being burnt out. A **great learner learns from everybody and everything. For him life is a teacher, a guru**. Let us now concentrate on various examples and analogies:

Wick: If we observe how the wick of a lamp functions, we will get many insights. It absorbs only the oil and no other impurities, like particles. It maintains the pace of burning, flickers at the start but settles down quickly giving a steady flame and produces light. Is it not analogous to a great learner in its qualities of absorbing only positivity and giving out only positivity?

Onion: We see that an onion has many layers; such is the human composition, made of physical, psychological and spiritual dimensions. Outer most layer is physical. As when the onion layers are peeled off, at the centre we find nothing, similarly our centre also comprises of a hollow, or nothingness.

Hollow Bamboo: We see that a good bamboo is hollow inside so that water can pass through it freely and it is strong outside so that it cannot be easily broken down. A true learner is also made of the same mettle

Cable: Electricity cable of good quality has least possible resistance so that output is very close to the input. Higher the resistance, higher is the transmission loss.

Commode/Urinal: The design is as such that it is humble enough to allow the waste to pass through it, thus keeping the house clean.

Example is to enable us to examine the truth in totality . . .

What is your Learning Style? You should have known a VAK model of learning i.e. Visual, Audio and Kinesthetic learning styles. Every individual has his own learning style. Some learn by analysis and some by synthesis.

What type of Learner you are?

- Sponge → Soaks everything, cannot discriminate between good and bad
- Funnel → Cannot retain anything
- Filter → Collects waste
- Thresher → Collects essence and throws away waste

What is the Biggest Barrier in Learning?

Ego is the biggest barrier in learning. When we are conditioned with ego and its various forms like age, gender, position, designation, experience, education, knowledge, caste/creed, and colour, etc. Our learning becomes skewed because we don't remain open-minded to receive anymore. For instance, a man, owing to his male ego, may not like to learn from a woman. An experienced VP of an organization may not like to take feedback from a new Management Trainee.

Beside psychological barrier, there are some physical barriers also, like non-conducive environment, language, accent, poor hearing ability, ill—health, poor communication skills significantly the listening skills, technological glitches etc.

Barrier can become a carrier if we invoke within us a 'never say die' warrior.

When I think of great learners, the first example that comes to mind is of the great archer Eklavya from *Mahabharata*, he proved that faith could enable one to master any form of art. Many times, we complain that we do not have that the necessary things, but time has proven that even the most deprived can be successful. Dr. B.R. Ambedkar, proved that knowledge is not a monopoly. Anybody and everybody can lead an exemplary life. His life is a great message for all true learners.

Being an 'empty cup' is not applicable for student but for a teacher also. If any teacher imposes this on students only then he/she is just a dictator/parrot who himself is full & closed. Isnt it a stupid ground rule of shutting down the quest of a student? And a kind of insecurity complex. 'What if student asks some tough Qs?' A great teacher himself is like an empty cup because he believes he is just a facilitator and not dictator. He creates a humble environment of 'transfer of learning' from teacher to student, student to teacher and among everybody in the class.

Only those who can Listen & Learn Truth can Speak & Share Truth!

Without honest Quest both the Student & Teacher are Waste. It must go on and on . . .

Na Kroadh se na Pratishodh se . . . Sacchi Shanti milti hai Swaym ke Shodh se aur Satya ke Bodh se . . .

Belief is an evolutionary seed that can grow into revolutionary Leaf provided we remove the weed of disbelief.

By Kiran Kurwade

Good Morning Tonic

- *One who can touch any heart can teach anyone. One who can listen to others can learn any lesson.*
- *Knowledge is when Knowing becomes a Living Edge,*
- *It's a great responsibility, use it judiciously at every Stage.*
- *When we start hearing "Unable" as "Enable", we become an Able in true sense . . .*
- *Gurur ko jo mita de woh Guru*
- *Jise buddhi ke astitva ka bodh nahi wah buddhu,*
  Aur jise astitva ke buddhi ka bodh ho wah buddha.

Space to write your own tonic

There is no Grave worse than
being a happy Slave, A Crisis Point
becomes a Rising Point for the Brave!

by Kiran Kurwade

3

Tonic for Great Self

When I am 'asleep' dreams seem real, when I am 'awake' reality seems like a dream.

Most of us know a great confusion of Chuang Tzu, a Chinese saint. Once at night he dreamt that he was a butterfly. When he woke up in the morning, he was in confusion that if man can dream of becoming a butterfly then it is also possible that butterfly can dream of becoming a man. He was unable to figure out whether now he was a man or a butterfly dreaming of becoming a man.

It is said that we are not human beings with spiritual experience, but spiritual beings with human experience.

Who or what I am? We know this famous story of an Eagle and Chicken. By chance, an eagle's egg rolls down to ground, somebody puts it among the Hen's eggs. Eventually it hatches and an eagle is born which grows along with the chicken and lives like a chicken. One day this eaglet is puzzled to see a flying eagle. **There is a sudden clash of thundering within him, a realization, and a kind of self-awareness. Self-Awareness is a mirroring experience of self**. He questions his guardian mother (hen) about the Eagle and his own flying possibilities.

Therefore, we are potentially like the eagle who can fly freely beyond borders. We are the free soul/spirit that dwells within our body. Are we challenging our limits, i.e. aiming high and achieving high continuously?

I feel true freedom is not in becoming any flying form but being a formless sky in which can take any form.

By Kiran Kurwade

Am I me or we? Scientifically there are so many living beings within my body then how can I say it is my body? Doesn't it belong to many others?

Another example: Sky is the experiencer and anything that flies in it the birds, the clouds, are the experiences. No cloud can be bigger than the sky and the beauty of sky lies in the flying birds, clouds, stars, planets, Sun etc. The holistic perspective would be the Sky (Experiencer) & the Clouds (Experience), and they complement each other.

When we remove every self-imposed label, only then we will be exposed to Truth and shall be truly available!

Womb to Tomb: From *Womb to Tomb* we always seek safety and miss experiencing the beauty of life. Once there lived a King, who was scared of death. He build a fort where nobody could enter. The fort had many walls and few doors. Later, he ordered to keep just a single door but remained scared, even though the fort was well guarded by the soldiers. He wanted some advice so he invited a Zen Master to help him. The Master said, *"You build so many walls without any doors in order to be safe. When you will close this single* door, then there will be no door left. This will become like a tomb, the safest place . . . no door so, no chance for anybody to enter or exit. This is nothing, but death."

The more we close all doors, the more we come closer to death; the more we open the doors, the more we live life. The closed doors are analogous to stubborn mindsets, conditioned lives, comfort zones and limited friend circles. Let us take a leap from a pond to the ocean, from limited to unlimited, from finite to infinite, from mortal to immortal, from stagnancy to growth. This is the foremost requirement of knowing and creating great self.

Great Leap is of a drop to ocean. Every drop has a ripple effect. Example, when a great freedom fighter dies while fighting for the great cause he becomes an inspiration for infinite beings, stays in their hearts as true love forever and thus becomes eternal. Unless we die to the past we cannot fly for the future. It's a transcendence of Me to We. The 'We' is all pervading and encompassing i.e. the entire universe. **Until we accomplish such eternity we live as restless souls.**

Let us understand how we can know through our few habits which showcase that we prefer to 'become' Great Self. Have you ever been sketched?

On weekends when we visit malls with friends and families, we come across the computerized sketch makers. Sometimes we do want to be sketched.

Imagine a *mystical painter* who makes amazing paintings, pictures, portrait of life. He makes three kinds of pictures of people.

- The picture who **You** are
- The picture which **others** see of you
- The picture which you want to **become**

So, which one would you want to paint yourself with? Most of us will opt for the third choice. The reflections behind this choice would be that being unhappy with our current faces and we would wish for better ones. Whenever we face a camera, we will ensure that our photo comes out best. Whenever we see a group photo, we first look for our own picture in the group.

We know that 'God is nowhere or God is now here,' depending on what we see, which is actually what we want to see. Sometimes, we find ourselves in the middle of nowhere and sometimes in the middle of nowhere, we find ourselves.

As long as we see our usual face, we remain at the surface, real fun starts when we face our faceless face.

Profound is found when you listen within you and around the same soundless sound.

By Kiran Kurwade

What is Self-Concept? We have just seen who we are and what our potentiality is. Let us understand more on how we can identify with the Self and consequently how our life is affected.

When we read SELF in reverse, we see it as FLES (Flesh). If we think we are flesh, we will miss the inner Flash. Flash attracts Flash and

Flesh attracts Flesh. When we identify ourselves as FLESH (body) alone, we are limited to body, hence with limited energy. Imagine a case where you play a football match after 15 years. Your family has come to the stadium to watch the game. You lose the match and soon after you lie on the ground very exhausted. If your team player comes and asks you to get up, you may get annoyed, as you are tired. However, if somebody comes and tells you that your little son in the stadium has fallen down, is injured, and needs immediate medical attention, will you run? Perhaps you will fly if you can. What makes you run when moments back you were unable to get up?

Your love for your child makes you run. Love is the driving force, a tonic indeed! You are not body alone, but also a heart (feeling), which gives e-motion and more energy. Imagine when we experience living as soul, our energy is much higher. Existence is energy and we have to match to its wavelength.

Let us explore and understand Self-Concept with the help of few analogies:

Water—When it is solid, it occupies less space. This is the egoistic state. When ego melts with the warmth of love, it can feel and reach many hearts like a flowing liquid and can move to more minute places. When it meditates and realizes no-thingness, it reaches equanimity and anonymity like the gaseous state of water, an almost invisible state at which it can reach higher and further places.

Milk—It contains butter, but it must be churned first to get butter. The solid part then settles down at bottom and the butter being lighter floats at the top.

Onion—The layers are synonymous to human behaviors, like the outermost is our behavior (action). When we start peeling the layers we can see the feelings, attitude, values etc. and at the center, i.e. innermost part, is hollow (no-thingness). We can re-visit such analogies in previous chapter *"Tonic for great Learner"*

Knowing Self is Good, Creating Self is Great

"All know the Way, but few actually walk it . . ." Bodhidharma

- **Trust yourself and Challenge yourself consistently**: Take risk, at least a calculated risk. *When you allow the body to merge, the soul will emerge.*
- **Be Now and Here:** Refer chapter *"Tonic of being Now & Here"*
- **Enquire Honestly and Holistically:** Turn within, practice interesting and inspiring meditation techniques, which will help you to experience truth.
- **Replace Good Habits with Great Habits**: **Have enough KASH**: Yes, if we want to enkash (encash) our truest self then we must master right **K**nowledge, **A**ttitude, **S**kill & **H**abit.
- **Be aware and beware of Ego**: When you know yourself truly then ego will be taken care, it is like you light a lamp and darkness disappears.

When we are with the FLOW of nature, We become a FLOWer of nature!

by Kiran Kurwade

Let's look at the two philosophies/spiritualities of India; Am the Absolute (Aham Brahmasmi) and Nothingness (Shoonya). Those ignorant of the first school of thought says, "Am the absolute or extra ordinary and others are ordinary/mediocre," while the enlightened says, "Anybody and everybody is bramha, in fact everything is bramha, only bramh is."

About the second school of thought (i.e. Nothingness), the ignorant says, "Everybody is nothing but I am something," while the enlightened says "World is just nothingness . . . I am no more but nothingness"

There is nothing like ego, which deceives so subtly. Ego takes many forms like age, experience, education, social status, knowledge, religion, caste colour etc. For instance, an old person may say to a child, "Don't teach me, I know more that you". If you wish, you can re-visit ego as a barrier in the chapter "Tonic to be a Great Learner"

"There are two rules on the spiritual path:

Begin and Continue . . ." Sufi saying

Good Morning Tonic

- SOUL is Spirit of Universal Love.
- As we believe, so we live.
- Let my body bend like the wind, heart flow like water, tears drop from the eyes like rains, mind remain stable like a rock and the soul serene, 'witnessing' everything like the sky . . .
- When I am 'asleep' dreams seem real, when I am 'awake' reality seems like a dream.
- When we remove every self-imposed label, only then we will be exposed to Truth and shall be truly available!
- When Truth calls, Ego falls.
- When ego drops, our true self crops.
- When Truth is realized on the way, then me, my & mine gets blown away. When we allow the body to merge, the soul will love to emerge.
- The more we become like a 'godown' (a place where unwanted things accumulate) the more we will go down.
- The nature of matter is to revolve and of non-matter is to evolve.

Imagine someone blindfolds when you want to see something interesting. The blindfold will make you restless. Similarly, we have blindfolded our inner eyes. Now imagine the restlessness inside yourself?

Space to write your own tonic

Invisible doesn't mean not visible but in-visible (visible inside).

By Kiran Kurwade

4

Tonic for Great Gift

Let us revisit a story of few Salesmen. Once, a sales team was on an adventure trip. At night they were relaxing at a riverside, when suddenly there was a flash of light and a voice said, "*There is a target for you . . . collection target*" Most of them on hearing this were put off and said, "*Even here there are talks of meeting targets . . . we are tired of targets*". The unknown voice said again "*Collect as many pebbles as you can and tomorrow some of you would be sad and some of you would be happy*". Somehow, the salesmen collected pebbles . . . most of them worked half-heartedly and few of them whole heartedly. Next morning most of them were sad, while few of them were happy as they realized the pebbles were not pebbles but diamonds. The story had a great revelation . . . the salesmen who had gathered more pebbles i.e. diamonds were those who had achieved higher Sales and Collection targets at their organization.

At times, we miss the real gifts. If a superfast train does not stop at your platform, it does not mean that it is not your train, it means either you are standing at the wrong platform or your platform is not big enough for such trains. Raise the bar!

Well, there is hardly anybody in the world who would not like to receive gifts. The gifts come in various forms.

Here we must ask few question to ourselves:

- What is the unique Gift/Strength that I have in me?
- How can I explore and get that Gift?
- What is the Gift that I can give to the world?

We are born gifted each one has his/her unique strength. Let us co-explore few common gifts we are endowed with:

Uniqueness is the biggest gift. Pick up two similar looking sand particles and take a microscopic view and you will see they are not same, two leaves of the same branch/tree are not alike and twins are never 100% identical. Each one and everything is unique in itself, because life is continuum, i.e. continuous change. Being unique is a gift since it gives us a scope to live life in a unique way, contribute in a unique way and leave behind a unique legacy. *Everything is unique in itself because it is ever changing; it is unique from one moment to another.*

Choice is another great gift to humanity. Let us revisit a story, which is quite ancient but also relevant to the present. Once a saint was taking a bath at a riverside, when he saw a scorpion being threatened by other animals. The saint without any second thoughts picked it in his palm and put at a safe place. While doing so the scorpion stung him. The next day again the saint came to take a bath and saw the scorpion in a similar situation and again saved him by taking it in his bare hand. The third day also the same thing happened. The disciples were amazed and confused at this act. One of them asked the saint why he took the scorpion in bare hand despite the scorpion stinging him. The saint replied; Animals work on instinct, they don't have any choice, in fact whenever I extended my hand for help . . . The scorpion got scared and it applied its defence mechanism to protect itself. However, I being a human have multiple options like-

- I would have killed it as it may cause harm to people coming at riverside especially the children
- I would have applied some brains and with the help of a stick would have dragged it away at safer place

- I would have just ignored it, taken my bath and would have walked away
- But I had this choice also that even **though it caused me pain but in return I will give only love & care**

The scorpion, being an animal did not give up its habit of spreading poison, so how can I as a human give up my nature of spreading love, be it for animal or person? Choice is the shadow of freedom, being free is our innate nature. What we win and what we lose depends on what we choose.

Freedom means free space, i.e. to dwell freely in space. If we maximize this space we will minimize the chances of getting victimized as regard to action and reaction or means and ends. Let us nurture the true nature. When we transcend to choice-less acceptance, we end all inner conflicts.

What we see in the world is a mere reflection of who are we. When we judge others, we in fact judge ourselves. Here I will share with you a story of two dogs, a happy dog and an angry dog. Both walk into a room at different times. One comes out wagging its tail happily and another comes out growling in anger. A person watching this goes into the room to check what could have made one dog happy and another angry. To his surprise, he finds the room was filled with many mirrors. The happy dog found thousands of dogs looking happily at him and the barking dog found thousands of dogs barking at him.

When we introspect spiritually, we realize that in fact everything is divinely planned for our own enlightenment.

In India it is said, "*Yahan kis ko mukammal jahan nahi milta, kisi ko zamin to kisi ko aasman nahi milta*" i.e. nobody gets everything at a given time. When we are young we have energy and time but no money, as adults we have energy and money but no time and as in old age we have money and time but no energy. However, there are exceptions, the secret of such winners are in the fact that the make best use of whatever is available. Thus, keep moving ahead for great purpose.

Anything and everything can be a great Gift. Let us look at an analogy: a tiny stem of a tree, which attaches the fruit to a branch.

It seemingly looks tiny and weak, but holds the much bigger fruit. The stem represents people who derive all the resources, processes, and knowledge from the Tree. Tree represents the society or an organization, and the Fruit can be the common people around us or customers. The 'stem' functions as GOD—Generator, Operator & Destroyer. The fruit is born on the stem, which supplies all nutrients, holds the fruit and one day breaks away when the fruit is ready and ripe. Breaking away is like giving freedom when it is ready. When a ripe fruit falls down, it's seeds spread all over, creating new trees. The destruction is pseudo-destruction, it is transformation, or we can say continuous creation or generation.

Believe in your Strengths, and Build your Strengths to Super Strengths so that nothing will Beat you.

We see every human being wants to grow in life. A teacher, a scientist, sportsman and almost everybody wants to be improve and do better in life. Significantly, business entrepreneurs and corporate professionals, why so we want to sustain forever and scale up endlessly? I feel there is something within us, which is *eternal* and *infinite*. Why we want to love and be loved? Because underlying the truth of existence is love. We are not human beings having spiritual experience, but spiritual beings having a human experience. It is said, *world suffers not because of the violence of bad people but because of the silence of good people*. Once we know our gifts, we have to utilize it judiciously. A great gift is a great power and a great responsibility indeed. We will explore in detail in the next chapter 'Tonic of great Purpose,' on how to actualize it.

GENIUS= Genie in Us. God and Ghost both lurk in us, whom we invoke is up to us.

By Kiran Kurwade

Good Morning Tonic

- ○ The moment you conquer your inner rival, it is the moment of self-revival.
- ○ Everybody we meet, every time we go through, every situation we face leads us to know our real face.
- ○ A fallen leaf comes back as butterfly to the plant. Let us follow our heart and work hard, we will get whatever we want.
- ○ Every Stone can be a Milestone
- ○ Greatest gift I can give to the world; myself becoming 'a way' instead of being 'away'

Space to write your own tonic

We can't stop a body by keeping a step on it shadow, how can we stop a soul by keeping a step on body? Isn't body a shadow of soul?

By Kiran Kurwade

5

Tonic for Great Purpose

Everyone is born for some Special Mission, and this is quite evident because there is nobody alive who does not think himself/herself as a special person.

In chapter 3, you became aware of who you are, and in chapter 4 you discovered your gifts. Now, let us know the purpose of these gifts.

It is said that every person is born for some purpose. In such a case, does a person create the purpose, or does the purpose create a person? Is it the dreamer who creates dreams or do the dreams create the dreamer, allowing them and actualize the dreams someday?

We cannot stop a body from moving by standing on its shadow, similarly it is not possible to stop a soul by standing on a body. Is not the body a shadow of one's soul? Let us now understand this aspect in a simple manner.

Most of us know a heart touching story of World War I. A soldier amid of great danger, puts his life at stake and goes on no man's land to meet his wounded and dying friend and try the best possible to save him. Soldier's senior tells him that it will be a big risk and not worthy enough to go there, as the person would have died. However, the soldier goes and experiences a great sense of satisfaction because the dying friend whispers in his ears, '*I know you would come . . .*" What would be the purpose of this soldier?

It is said the safest place for ship is harbor but that's not it made for.

Only great Self can see great Purpose, utilizes great Gift and shall make the great Shift. They proved the Junoon (willpower) can change the Genes

"agar paristhiti badalne se manasthiti badal sakti hai to manasthiti badalne se parishthiti kyun nahi badal sakti?"

We often say 'I know . . .' but actually we don't know i.e. we may have some of the knowledge but not the complete knowledge. We may be good in outer knowledge but not the inner. No wonder we live in tension and find difficult to stop it's extension.

Few people did it; be it the saints or soldiers, astronauts or artists, traders or teachers. Were they extra ordinary? What makes them unbeatable? The great purpose indeed . . .

This is a story about three sales professionals. There was an MBA student doing his internship project at one of the consumer electronics companies. In an employee satisfaction survey he came across three sales persons in a multi brand showroom recently opened at a remote and rural place. He introduces himself to the 1st sales person who was looked like a confused courier boy and asked "What is your experience in sales?" The salesperson reacted angrily" Can't you see am completely drenched in rain and about to enter the shop, please don't ask me anything". After some time the student sees the second sales person who looks stressed, is wearing good clothes but sounds tired, and he asks the same question. The sales person replies submissively that he is just fulfilling his duties/JD-KRA by visiting the showroom for sales & collection target achievement, in order to earn good money. Eventually the student meets another salesperson who looked calm and relaxed, and he asked the same questions. The third person replied, "Am here to enable people to 'experience change' in their lives, primarily in the education front. The villagers will surely be entertained by watching movies and serials, but the younger viewers would watch various educative channels and receive education that would help them to make their lives prosperous and peaceful.

All the 3 salespersons must be getting the same salary, same JD/KRA but the question is who has a higher purpose and hence the most productive? Thus, a great man is always purpose-centric, whether he is dealing with education, power, automobile, telecom, consumer durable etc.

My understanding is that the ignorant who works only for money and livelihood says, "My work is my bread and butter", and the enlightened who works for higher purpose says, "My work is my breath and everyone is my brother." Why Breath? Work is as important and integral as Life. Why Brother? We all are the children of Almighty and Almighty is One. The 3rd Millennium belongs to the leaders who are scientific as well as spiritual.

How to actualize our Purpose?

Actualizing the great Purpose makes it necessary to imbibe tonics for being in the Now, great Self, great Gift, great Intelligence, great Learner, great Solution, great Team, great Relationships, great Leader, great Professional and great Change Maker. These are various chapters of the book, which will give more clarity.

Knowing greater Self will unleash great Gift and greater will be the Purpose. Let us recall the various states of water mentioned in 'Tonic for great Self' like solid, liquid and vapor. In chapter 'Tonic for great Learner', there are few analogies like learning from the role of Wick (lamp), Hollow Bamboo, Electricity Cable and even the commode. We can know their purpose and learn to find out ours.

Since, greatness is about Inner Journey; hence, to bring out the great Purpose let us briefly look at few more analogies and certain action points.

With rains, many trees flower easily, but it is rare to see a *Delonix regia (species of a flowering plant)*, which in India is called as

Gulmohar. It blooms with beautiful flowers during the scorching heat of summer and gives us few lessons-

- Standing in scorching heat, other trees become dry. The leaves give up and die but *Gulmohar* remains fresh.
- Stressed travelers upon seeing Gulmohar feel relaxed and happy. There is something within the seed (Inner) of *Gulmohar*, which conquers the heat (Outer).
- Similarly friends, in business context it is easy to achieve our goals when the environment is favorable but only few like *Gulmohar* don't give up and delight the internal and external customers even during tough time.

When it rains, the birds take refuge in their nests to protect themselves but it is only the king of birds, i.e. Eagle, which flies over the scary clouds. If we remain content with good performance, then how will we stand out with great performance? and how will we achieve our great purpose? We know the universal law . . . law of attraction . . . . like attracts like.

We know the universal law . . . law of attraction . . . like attracts like. **Significantly, whatever we like, it should be soulful only then it will be powerful to sustain else it can die.**

Have you made your Dream Vision Board and placed it at your home? and ensured Positive Affirmations? It is imperative to move from SMART to SMARTER Goal . . .

Engage = Young Age

"Its not enough to be busy, so are the ants, the question is what are we busy about?" Henry David Thoreau.

Hence I feel, **Engage** is **Young Age** i.e. we are never late to engage. Nature of mind is to engage, if we don't engage with positive, it will engage with negative. And that which is done in haste is often waste. Infact the wise makes the best out of waste.

BUSY = BE EASY

A great purpose oriented can't afford to say that he is busy, he has to make every task so easy that even being so busy he enjoys and thus achieves the goal easily.

SMARTER = Specific, Measurable, Achievable, Realistic, Time Bound, Enjoyable & Revenue generating.

How to make a dream vision board?

- ○ Visualize your goals . . . short term and long term . . . personal and professional. Think Big!
- ○ Write your goals on the board or on a paper and pin it up.
- ○ Ensure the goals are in present tense. For instance, "I am, (your name) very rich and live in a big house, I am very healthy, I am highly respected in the market etc. Like attracts Like, so richness attracts richness. Hence, we have to be grateful what we have and feel rich about it. The richness has to be ambitious and not complacent so that it attracts more richness. Richness can be of wealth, health or great knowledge.
- ○ Decorate the board with inspiring visuals, quotes, taglines etc.
- ○ Avoid negative words including No, Not etc.
- ○ Early morning when you get up, have a look at it, then the whole thought process would proceed accordingly.
- ○ At night before sleeping look at it gratefully, because thoughts go deeper into the sub-conscious mind and tends to create a deep effect.
- ○ Feel your goals, have faith and pursue passionately.
- ○ Stay Focused, Stay Happy, be a Winner every Day. Move from **Can I to I Can**

Here I quote Thomas Alva Edison, *"I did not fail 1000 times but found out the 1000 ways which don't work"*

Any Role without Goal is like a Body without Soul.

By Kiran Kurwade

Action. Action. Action

"Action is the foundation key to all success . . ." Pablo Picasso

In India there is a famous saying "*Waqt se pehle aur kismet se zyada yahan kisi ko kuch nahi milta*" meaning here nobody gets anything before his time, and nothing more than his fate allows. If we follow this then we will not be able to transcend our good life to great life. On contrary, we will become so complacent that we will fall in the abyss of happy slavery. Since we will not work hard and make any efforts, there will not be any progress in any dimension of life. We will be born poor and we will die poor, by poverty I do not mean just in terms of financial aspects, but spiritual also. What legacy are we going to leave for our next generations?

Dream Vision Board will help you to visualize your goals but you have to mobilize yourself to achieve it. Once lived a person who always used to pray to God to bless him with a lottery win and make him a millionaire. One day God appeared to him and said, "At least buy a lottery ticket"

Such is our state, where we think a lot, make many plans and but are unable to achieve it. In the corporate world, it is observed that plans are very well made but the organizations bleed in operations i.e. the execution. In our chapter *"Tonic for Great Intelligence"* we will deal in detail the factors that prevent us to action our goals. Briefly, we need to understand the mind, heart, soul, body and intelligence, especially the heart, which is the faculty of motivation and soul or spirit of the values.

Anyway, when we get bogged down in life then we must REMEMBER the most happiest/touching moments, which will give us strength to knock down any barrier. Actually, we all are MEMBERS of a common and divine club called life. Sometimes when we forget this, we just need to close our eyes, feel the vibes and we will RE-MEMBER again the true meaning of life.

Until we have an EXCUSE to FAIL, we cannot USE our greatest strength to SAIL.

Who are the STARS? Get Tonic from STARS

Hope some of you have the hobby of sky gazing and observing the stars. Our life is also like a sky, sometimes cloudy, sometimes clear. Who are the STARS? Can we say they are the one who Shine Tirelessly and Radiate Soulfully.

Can we call them the achievers of Shining Targets amid Receding Situations because they never give up their Spiritedly Travel At Revolutionary Speed?

Often they are testified (visible) when the environment is dark i.e. tough, traumatic & tiring.

Some objects shine during the day like glass and few at night like the Moon, that means they depend on reflected light, while stars have their own light. The real stars are those beings/non-beings who have ignited their inner light and have become the light itself . . . they are ever shining . . . it is our inability to see them all the time.

45

Jisne 'aaj' ko jeeta usne har 'taj' ko jeeta. Bhagyawadi sitaren (zodiac stars) dekhta reh jata hai aur karmwadi ek mahan sitara (star performer) ban jata hai . . .

The one who believes in fate keeps thinking about the zodiac stars and the one who believes in himself gives the best performance, thus becomes a great star.

When nothing is sure, everything is possible. In India we have a common saying, *'Whatever happens, happens for the best . . .'* then the *karmwadi* (man of deeds) chooses to operate from the very best i.e. the soul.

Once you keep your feet down then nothing defeat you down because the real fight is not between you and others but you and yourself.

By Kiran Kurwade

Good Morning Tonic

- *WINNER= WIN+INNER. The one who has won his inner self can conquer outer self*
- *Jo chhodta nahin koi kasar wahi to lata hai asar!*
  Agar man mein ho zeal to door nahin manzil!

- *If a superfast train of big opportunity doesn't stop at our station it doesn't mean its not our train but either we are at wrong station or our station is too small for such trains.*
- *When the roots are strong, the trees will dance in the storm. And when the roots dance in the storm they have to become strong.*
- *When it becomes our nature to keep the graph of life rising after every fall, then our signature becomes an inspiring autograph for all.*
- *It's the Pace with Grace that wins the Race*
- *DOOR & DOER are made for each other. When the 'O' of Opportunity in DO'O'R is Executed by 'E' it becomes DO'E'R.*
- *There is nothing to win and nothing to lose, when there is no-thing to choose.*
- *If we tie the rope of life with hope, then death is a lie. Life is an adventure, respect its nature. Life will find its way do not let your faith run away. Without suffering and pain, the safar (journey) of life is like ocean without water.*
- *Whenever I fight against the "Wrong" I become more "Strong."*

Space to write your own tonic

Illusion is Ill Vision.

by Kiran Kurwade

6

Tonic for Great Intelligence

If we can have great dreams, great devotion and a great sense of divinity then we shall co-create great designs . . .

Today, with the help of scientists, doctors and engineers we may make our life advanced and luxurious. Through genetic engineering, we are creating intelligent living beings and engineers are creating magnificent skyscrapers. In addition, many technological designs are being created. However, are we evolving? We can increase life span, stop ageing and almost become immortal but will it ensure world peace? Will it end the mass of suffering?

Until now, we have been exploring self-realization and actualization. We feel that we know everything. 'I know' . . . 'been there and done that,' 'Hello! What is new?' A majority of the people have this mind-set. The one who claims he knows everything, in reality doesn't know much. We do not trust anybody not even our own selves. We doubt everything and our doubts reflect our ignorance.

There is a gap between knowing and doing. In Marathi, there is a famous saying "*Kalata pan valat nahi*," meaning I know but somehow I am unable to do. We know that Knowing is Mind and Doing is Body. Unfortunately, most of us take pride and pleasure in BMW i.e. Body Mind World only, and miss out on other two important dimensions, viz. Feeling is Heart and Being is Soul/Spirit.

If we want to plug the gap then we will have to find the tonic for heart and soul, only then the person will become completely intelligent

49

or holistically intelligently. In fact, universe has great intelligence, the stars the planets etc. Whatever we observe in nature, every tree, every bird, every mountain, every river, every desert etc. has intelligence. And everything is inter-connected with one common and higher intelligence. Once we crack that higher intelligence, we become holistically or greatly intelligent.

Let us re-visit our existing knowledge on multiple intelligences. We are very well aware of these various intelligences. There is plethora of books available on it.

Mind=IQ (Intelligence Quotient), Heart=EQ (Emotional Quotient), Soul =SQ (Spiritual Quotient) and Body=PQ (Physical Quotient). Unfortunately, most of us think that IQ the only intelligence that is the basic and necessary.

By classification of various intelligences, I do not mean human brain contains just IQ. In fact it is a great gift that contains various other faculties including emotional and spiritual aspects. Having said, it does not mean that brain is the only seat of intelligence; every organ, every cell has its intelligence. All intelligences in turn are inter-connected and driven by a higher intelligence. Can we say that IQ is Mind Power, EQ is Willpower, SQ is Purpose Power and PQ is Physical Power?

IQ is misinterpreted as mere mental ability, by most of us. I remember my school days, when a student scored good marks in science and mathematics, he was looked upon as a bright student having high IQ student, while a student with an inclination towards humanities and possessing love and compassion, was considered having lower IQ.

May I quote Albert Einstein *"Everybody is a genius. But if you judge a fish by its ability to climb a tree, it will live its whole life believing that it is stupid."*

Is a person with a good memory and fast calculating capabilities the only intelligent student? What if this student becomes a good engineer but turns egoist and selfish? If he fails to connect with people, and does not empathize with the feelings of others around him? Cannot remain devoted to anyone? He does not make and maintain win-win relations and hence cannot get good business results. He does not want to contribute anything to the society, lives a stressed life, and during retirement becomes a loner. *People do not care how much you know unless they know how much you care for them.*

Holistic intelligence is all encompassing, all-inclusive and all pervading. We are interconnected. In order to explore holistic intelligence, let us understand its various faculties or sub-intelligences, which have been already stated above; IQ, EQ, SQ and PQ. Let me reinstate, 'IQ' mentioned here in my table of classification is only the ability to think.

We are living in the 21st century, we deal in 'Dreams', dream big . . . achieve big. Who can dream big? Dreaming reflects capacity of thinking, imagination, visualization, information, experiences, analyzing, co-relating so on and so forth. Human beings are dreaming beings. Dreaming is the basic quality of human beings. It is thinking with pictures. As you dream, so you become. Without dream, we cannot create any design. How many of us are able to actualize our dreams? Dream without action is a daydream. We have discussed about the Dream Vision Board in chapter '*Tonic for great Purpose*'

4D Intelligence: 4D is not 4-Dimensional Intelligence but a holistic intelligence that comprises all possible dimensions. In information age, we have abundant information or ideas; hence, I would like to term the basic intelligence—Intellect Quotient (IQ) as **Dream Quotient (D1). The Dream Quotient is about conscious dreaming. We know dreams surface out the sub-conscious thoughts and latent desires. Dreams transcend time zones and not only see the past but glimpse the future (intuition).**

One who is emotionally intelligent has to have the devotion. Devotion to self, to people, hence I would like to term it as Devotion Quotient (D2). Devotion reflects commitment, promise, sensitivity to others' feelings, driving force.

Spirit and soul have been widely used and it reflects divinity. The underlying essence, the common denominator, hence I would like to term it as Divinity Quotient (D3). It is about great purpose, inter-dependence, oneness and global peace.

The body is a design, human body is a kind of design and similarly any other animate or inanimate bodies have certain design. Machines have certain design. Universe is a great design. Design is the delivery, manifestation, structure, system, solidity and reality hence I would like to term it as Design Quotient (D4).

4D = D1, D2, D3 & D4 together is the Holistic or Great Intelligence; it is all encompassing, all—inclusive and all pervading.

Let us co-explore the various intelligences present in human beings on the following dimensions:

- **Understand** each type of intelligence.
- Know the **characteristics** of a person possessing such intelligence.
- Know the **benefits** of all types of intelligences in our personal and professional lives.
- Know possible ways to **enhance** each type of intelligence.
- **Align** each type of intelligence and thus get a tonic for great or holistic intelligence.

Please Note: The intelligence concept and the table mentioned here are purely as conceived by self, Kiran Kurwade. It has nothing to do with any existing study on these intelligences. The entire concept can be wrong or have a biased perception, since it is the writer's personal view. However, if it helps you to think holistically and enables you to move towards a great life then my work is fruitful, and I will be grateful.

4D Intelligence as conceived by Kiran Kurwade			
D1	D2	D3	D4
Dream Quotient	Devotion Quotient	Divinity Quotient	Design Quotient
It's the basic intelligence. An ability to observe and absorb. Observation can be two ways; wider and deeper i.e. observing many things and/or one thing with great in-depth. Dreaming and observing go together. Dreaming is thinking in pictures.	An ability to sense emotions in various beings and respond positively. Generous and kind heartedness. Devotion is the base for all relationships. It is the index of sensitivity. Greater the devotion, greater the win-win relations. Associations, organizations.	An ability to remain in touch with higher self as a pure witness. Compassionate towards all at all times. Divinity is the purity, the serenity, the peace. The un-manifest lurks in all the beings and non-beings.	An ability to manifest the ideas, dreams, desires i.e. the design. Hence, to keep the surrounding and structures as strong as possible. Maintaining body as healthy and energetic.
Characteristics			
Good dreamer because good thinker, strategist, planner, analytical, knowledgeable (informative), good memory, an eye for detail, facts & figures oriented, microscopic, works out 'pros & cons'. Highly logical. Profit oriented. Their basic motivation is individual success.	Devotion surpasses logic. They can empathize others, sensitive, doesn't get bogged down easily, has good relations, good at networking, motivated and can motivate others, good team leaders. They are people and their values oriented. Their motivation is people, respect and dignity.	Divinity seekers, Truth seekers. Peace loving. Conscience matters a lot to them. They are very conscious, compassionate, calm, composed, serene, unbiased, meditative, looks at big picture, speaks oneness. They are principle/ human values/peace oriented. They are self-motivated and practice equanimity.	They are good in delivering, creating a design, manifesting, crystallizing the ideas. Energetic, physically fit and can sustain pressure of working long hours, fast in action. Can endure physical environment and exhibits good stamina. They are healthy body oriented. Environment plays imp role in their motivation.

Dream Quotient	Devotion Quotient	Divinity Quotient	Design Quotient
WIIFM—What is in it for me?			
Its an information age, hence such people can lead the show and prosper faster. The teams and organizations prefer to have such people. Their domain knowledge and expertise has an extra edge over competition. It's the basic intelligence which can enable them to compute and calculate faster and predict based on the past and ongoing trends.	We live in families, groups, teams, organizations, society hence connecting and having win-win relationship is very important. Such people with high devotion can feel the feelings of others and thus make long lasting and fruitful relations and associations. Almost every advertisement has emotional elements.	Being higher principle oriented they tend to contribute thru great vision and mission. They are the great mentors for teams and organizations. Their long term and holistic and all-inclusive approach helps the people around to co-create and co-evolve. Their need is strongly felt now and in coming years it will be felt more. They are the hope for world peace. Most of the real charity missions is the work of such leaders.	Dream without Action is like a day dream. They are the task masters, action heroes, the doers. They are good in operations and passionate to win. They take great efforts. They contribute immensely by translating the vision of any organization into reality. They achieve the targeted design/structure/ solidity/expression
How to Enhance?			
Anything which can stretch the intellect, enable to think more, dream new can enhance this intelligence. Exposure to new areas, places, cultures can be a good acceleration. Practicing IQ tests, playing such games which can make you think, solve and design new case studies.	Empathizing is the key of this intelligence. HOPE stands for Help Others, Pain Ends. It is not only about making new and more relations but maintaining the old relations as happy as possible. Know the art of gifting. Example, Such people will never miss out a chance to delight others on special occasions like b'days, anniversaries etc.	Conscientious, Conscious and Compassionate living through meditations or prayers or anything which can connect to higher self and brings you true peace. Recognize your strength and utilize it for the best of as many beings possible. Live a clean and purposeful life and be a change maker . . .	Relaxing, managing stress. Getting physically engaged. Work outs, gymnasiums, jogging tracks, sports etc. Great leaders involve themselves at front end works and create designs. Yoga is widely practiced. Over indulgence of body is the barrier. Eating right diet, the supplements, regular health checks keeps it going great.

Am I an Intuitive Executive? To be intuitive is higher form of intelligence. Anybody can tell what is happening currently, but sensing the future shows great intelligence. We know the story of two frogs. When they placed in two separate containers of milk, one dies because it gives up saying that it is habituated to only water, can swim only in water, and thus cannot face the change. Another frog does not gets bogged down with the forced change and continues swimming in the container and in the due course the milk due to good churning turns into a lump of butter. The sweat of the frog too contributes to the curdling of the milk. The frog sits meditatively on the top of the lump and leaps out of the container to freedom when opened. In fact, inside the container he was already in a state of freedom.

We have witnessed the Mahatmas . . . the prison was unable to imprison them and they made the best of their abilities . . . . many became well-known writers while being in the jail. Every wall is a door for them.

How can I trust my hunches and become successful Intuitive Executive/Manager? Because existence is entropy (randomness), many factors attribute to the success, as regard achieving targets. What does one do when a game is changed? How to emerge as a winner?

What—Why—How—Whom of 4D Intelligence: What is to be achieved is to **Design Intelligence (D4)**, it is crystallizing the abstract, manifesting the dream, and translating thought. If it is not developed, then we fail to give a backbone to the concepts, and ideas. **Why** indicates the **Divinity Intelligence (D3)** i.e. the purpose, higher the purpose, higher the intelligence eventually leading to oneness. If it is not adequate then we lack peace and compassion. 'How' is answered by **Dream Intelligence (D1)**, the ingredients are multi-dimensional thinking, planning and strategizing. If it is not adequate then we will not able to think rationally. **Whom** means the specific person as people vary from place to place, culture to culture. It should comprise other living beings also. When we do not have **Devotion (D2)** then we suffer on loneliness and often have small and volatile friend circle.

Intelligences work in simultaneity, like various systems work, e.g. digestive, respiration, blood circulation etc. However, Spiritual Intelligence is the centre, if you focus on it, then rest of the intelligences will fall into place. When you align BMW (Body Mind World) with heart and soul then nothing can stop you from achieving your goals. Invoke the soulful driver of your BMW (Body Mind World) to drive a new race; a pace with grace wins the race.

Naturalise yourself with the new surroundings. Look from multiple levels, perspectives and dimensions. Be clear on imaginary and real obstacles

Self-observation without any prejudices is highest intelligence as echoed by many spiritual practitioners. I think, self-witnessing is not just aware of self but self plus everything around. I become so exclusive that everything becomes inclusive.

Without Divinity, the dreams and designs are skewed and superficial. Divinity is the light . . . a guiding light.

May I quote Thoreau, *"Our truest life is when we are in dreams awake."*

The person whose heart (attitude) is great will use the brain (aptitude) and reach the success (altitude) constructively.

Have you had your Tea? Yes, TEA can stand for Thoughts (mind), Emotions (heart) and Actions (body), a stimulant for great intelligence in a human being.

Good Morning Tonic

- *Great Intellect is not to just deflect the outer object, but to conquer the inner defect and reflect +ve effect*
- Imagination is about Image i.e. whatever we imagine it will be an image.
- *Human design is like a Guitar, music cannot come if the strings are too tight or too loose. Our mind strings have become too tight and the body too loose. We have to balance the strings; loosen the mental strings and tighten the body strings. (Source: Osho's Discourse)*
- *Life is a greatest paradox . . . it is together one & many . . . universal & unique . . . particle & wave . . . body & soul . . . tears & smile . . . good & bad . . . in fact its multi-colour . . . shades of one colour . . . rainbow of single light.*
- *The profound is found when you hear in you and around the same soundless sound*
- *Still Mind and Steel Body can conquer anything and anybody. However, that which plays an integral role is the heart and soul.*

Space to write your own tonic

7

Tonic for Great Solution

I wonder how,
Seed turns from tree to flower and then back to seed again,
Ocean becomes cloud, rain and back to ocean again,
Consciousness becomes mind, meditates and turns into consciousness
again!

Have you switched on the Light? One night, a family after watching a movie returns home, father opens the door of house and stumbles into the room. He angrily blames that the housekeeper doesn't keep the things properly. His little child says, *"Father, it's your mistake . . . you did not switch on the lights. If you had first switched on the lights, you would have seen things clearly and not stumbled."* So put on the flame and avoid the blame.

With the rise of technology, we are good at switching on the external lights but often forget to switch on the Inner Light. Unless we do not do that, we dwell in the dark. Once we accomplish that, then we see every bit of universe lit up with light.

Dark is not the opposite of light but the absence of light; fighting with dark is futile just bring light and dark is no more. In fact my I feel, everything is lit it is our inability to see the light. When we are able to see our inner light, we will see light everywhere and everything clearly.

Holistic Approach: Suppose you are blindfolded and taken to an unknown forest, left all alone and you do not know the way out. How will you try to get out of the forest? You may try the following:

- Shout . . . Help! Help! Expecting somebody around will hear your voice and help you.
- If you know the direction and have a compass with you then you will follow the direction with the help of compass. In case of day time you may follow the sun and during night follow the position of the stars.
- You may look for any footpath created by people walking.
- You may even look for the footprints of animals that might lead to a water reservoir etc.
- If you have torchlight, you may flash it expecting somebody sees to it.
- You may walk and mark the signs on trees so that you do not come back to same place.
- You might listen to any noise of traffic and walk towards that direction.
- You may climb the tallest tree and from up there you could see things clearly.

Any option may work out. However, climbing a tallest tree is surely better than the other options.

The main problem is our restricted vision that disallows us to see things clearly and completely. At the ground level or from our standpoint the vision is limited to only few meters, but from the tallest tree, the vision is widened from there one can see up to many kilometres. As long as we exist at a narrow level, we say it is a problem, and the moment we widen our bandwidth, the problem disappears, like when we bring a light the darkness disappears. The more we rise psychologically or spiritually, we have a greater bandwidth at which we can view a bigger picture. This approach is like a helicopter view. We have to enlarge our bandwidth marginally on a daily basis and we shall have a greater bandwidth encompassing larger concerns. The beauty is that all concerns bottle down to a common base.

It is observed in organizations also. A salesperson or an executive from any department will have his departmental point of view, but the CEO has a bigger view as he can see all the departments.

Seeing through the Lens of existence: First, exchange Perspectives; secondly, whenever we have a problem it is the result of our biased views. A person wearing green glass will see the world as green, and the one wearing blue will see it as blue. Both are right in their own perspectives. Problem starts when one claims he is right and other wrong. Then there is conflict, confusion and chaos.

One has to remove his coloured glasses and wear the other coloured ones, so that he can see from other's perspective too. Empathy is often referred to as putting ourselves in other's shoes. First, we have to remove our shoes i.e. change our mindset or perceptions and feel the other person's pain. Therefore, it is feeling the pain (problem) of another person and providing the right shoes (solution). Before I ask for divinely help, my task is to totally unmask myself.

Root is the Route: Thirdly, imagine a case of a little child who does not know much about plants and if you ask him to water the plant, he may water the branches or leaves etc. that which is visible. He does not know about the roots because they are hidden or not visible from outside, while we adults know, it is the roots that need watered plant growth. Even if we want to get rid of the tree we have to uproot it, cutting the branches may regenerate the branches and leaves, and the tree grows back. the same can be said about the problems and solutions in our day-to-day lives.

Don't fumble be humble; when we focus on problem, the solutions stumble but when we focus on solution the problems tumble . . .

We have to identify the symptoms, the root cause, the solutions and implement them intelligently: There are many scientific techniques to identify and solve. The one who upgrades continuously with the relevant techniques succeeds. Work that cannot be done manually must be accomplished using the help of technology. You know the available management science techniques for solving a problem like Brain Storming, Fish Bone, Root Cause Analysis, SWOT Analysis, Paired Comparison, the 5Ws, 5S, PDCA Cycle etc. The approach should be Diagnostic and Remedial, so that we clearly bifurcate whether the problem is related to Man, Machine, Method, Material or Money. It is observed that a major reason in not getting a right solution is the lack of KASH i.e. right knowledge, right attitude, right skill and right habit of solving a problem.

As for example, it is our common experience that when we are sitting in a train that has halted and look at other moving trains, we feel that our train is moving. However, when we look at the platform, we realize it is the other train that is actually moving and not ours. Watching from the third perspective will give us the real view.

Never count on immediate success. We should be short term enough to beat the present and long term enough to meet the future.

When we re-visit Chemistry, it says Solution is a homogenous mixture of solute and solvent. Solute is a substance dissolved in another substance called solvent what constitutes the major fraction. Characteristics of the solution are more or less of the solvent. Who is the solute, solvent and the solution in our corporate world? I feel, Solute is day to day Problems (Challenges), Solvent is the People (Roles) and Solution is the Life (System/Culture). Unless we people do not increase our solubility i.e. acceptance, adaptability and affection towards each other how can we become a great solvent and lead to a great solution? Solution is the System we co-create.

So, Solvent (People) plays an important role to dissolve the Solute (Challenges) and make a Solution (System) which is by the people, of the people and for the people.

Essentially, Solution has to be continuously Upgraded, Uniting & Universal. It is not merely to Go through but to Grow through.

We have to Move from egoistic 'I' to detailed 'Eye'.

Black & White are not opposite of each other but composite of each other.

By Kiran Kurwade

Good Morning Tonic

- *A really great person is not when he talks of big things but when he understands small things . . . works on it and makes great things happen*
- *When we view the Truth of Inner world, we shall have a Real view of Outer world.*
- *Higher we 'Arrange' higher we 'Range'.*

Space to write your own tonic

LIFE stands for Love Inspires Freedom Everywhere.

By Kiran Kurwade

8

Tonic for Great Relationship

RESPECT= Re Spect i.e. to see again

We are getting so busy in Touch Screens and forgetting the touch of Living Beings. In the same house, son wishes his father "Happy B'day" on FB or sends an SMS. Why he cannot step out from his room and simply hug? There is a difference between human being and being human.

Once a girl was on the pilgrimage, it was a hilly region. While climbing a hill she carried her younger brother. One of the Sadhus (a sage) looking at the small girl said, "*Why don't you take some rest and put the child aside. You must be feeling cumbersome due to the weight of the child*". Girl responded, "*Sadhu ji does your head, legs, hands feel like an extra weight for you?*" Sadhu said, "*No . . . they are my body parts*". Girl said, "*So is my brother . . . he is my heart . . . how he can be a burden for me. I love him . . . in fact I get energy through his presence, his innocent touch and voice . . . his warmth is the source of my energy.*"

Similarly, be it family, friends, customers or colleagues we have to feel each other. Togetherness creates great harmony and due to a harmonious approach, we shall achieve our goals with ease.

Why children most of the time are seen fresh and energetic? For them there is NO difference between home and outer world. The whole world is home for them. During travel we tend to get mental fatigue and stress but children remain fresh because we become hygiene conscious and think the surrounding is not so good. A feeling of being separate from home weakens us. The idea of 'other' disintegrates us. In addition, the children do not think or worry much. Thinking with worry consumes lot of our energy.

Until we exist in piece we cannot attain peace, we have to move from being *jealous to zealous.* With deep gratitude, if we meditate then we realize that everything is divinely planned for our own co-evolution *We have moved from Cart to Car . . . but remained away from each other's hearts, only Love and Love alone can bring us closer.*

Be the Curve, Be the Verve: We know from our school days that if force is applied on an egg in an upright position, it becomes very difficult to break it. According to Scientific logic, this is owing to its shape, which evenly distributes the weight and pressure as seen in domes and cathedrals. A dome can hold enormous space and energy without any supporting angle or pillar. Similarly, our head also has a curve accumulating divine energy. The curve has great latent energy. The best curve I feel is the curve of a smile, which brings life to self and many frustrated ones. Normally, in a public place we see strangers looking at each other in an unfriendly manner. Why?

At workplace, we often experience this lack of smile, especially on Mondays. *How to beat the Monday Blues?* Invoke a curve (smile) and be the verve (enthusiastic energy). So convert the Monday Blues into Monday Magic. A smile of a baby gives great bliss to the mother, so should the smile of a team player energise the team leader and vice versa. When we look at an egg, we realize that when power is invoked from within a life begins, and when a force is applied from outside a life ends. This is an analogy of Self-Motivation. Those who have found their inner self they move from Motivation to Self-Motivation. Emotion is an energy, which is contagious, spreads smile, happiness and life.

"If we cannot love the person whom we see, how can we love God whom we cannot see?" Mother Teresa

What is a prime barrier for Great Relationship @Work/Business? Ego has various subtler forms. Never judge people with your GLASS. **GLASS** stands for **Gender—Looks—Age—Show-Off—Status**

Gender bias can be a barrier. Women can be good performers as business representatives, as well as the potential business partners/dealers. **Looks**—Appearances vary from person to person, geography to geography and culture to culture. With the rise of internet and mass media magic, the world has become flat. Nuclear families, high disposable incomes and luxurious lifestyles have led to multi-level life. Even in businesses, this prevails among primary, secondary and tertiary customers. A villager may look poor by appearance but may have power in terms of money, networking, etc.

Age—People who are always in the learning mode keep growing at any age. Lethargy inhibits most of us in failing to achieve our goals. Age is no bar for all learning aspirants. Regarding business partners, never under estimate the youngsters as well as the elders.

Show—Off—People often show off that which they normally lack. Pre-empt positively and judge judiciously. Regarding business partners, beware of false promises and fake proposals. Through reliable references, cross check their socio-economic status and capabilities as successful business partners.

Status—Designation, position, past success/failures, socio-economic factors, culture, caste/creed no longer hold any substance. Merit matters. Regarding network expansion, instead of depending on few channel partners, it's better to add more new partners.

Empathy is often defined as putting self in other's shoes and in this context, we don't remove our own shoes but try to enter into other's shoes, resulting in tearing off their shoes. I have another paradigm of Empathy . . . Can't I put aside/forget my feet and shoes completely? Can't we feel other's feet (pain) and give him/her the right shoes (solution)? "Treat others the way they want to be treated" and not the way you want to treat them.

So, 'OUR' is the need of an Hour. We should realize and execute the POWER of OUR. It also brings out the great concept of Inter-dependence. We are not here to compete with each other but to complete each other. It does not matter how long we Live, what matters is how well we get along with each other while we Live.

Buddha said, "*Expectations is the cause for all sufferings*" It is a great truth. Relationship means expectations, be it a personal or professional relationships. We have to accept each other and if at all to expect than expect the unexpected. It is not easy and may seem impractical but it is true that maintaining a relationship requires great deal of patience and empathy. Any relationship exists in a win-win format; an employee's winning expectation is good remuneration, recognition and respect from the organization, and an organization's winning expectation is essential returns from the employee. Life is not like a football, cricket or any other game, where one party wins and other loses. Life is about win-win relationships. If an employee does not get what he is supposed to get, he resigns and if an organization does not get the expected returns then it terminates the employee, a fair deal indeed. The same can be said about company-customer, husband-wife, father-son and other relationships, where the expectation levels may vary. In a fast changing world, when we closely observe self and realize that that what we like in the morning may not be so desirable in the evening, we experience change. Then why we should not expect a change from others? They are also experiencing changes. Exchange the change and co-create a great life.

There is something which integrates us, it converts every cry into joy . . . it can never die and it has to be ONE, therefore its COMMON. When the Sky is tearful it rains, the Sun feels its pain and makes it smile in the form of a Rainbow. Be a Rainbow Smile in someone's Tears. This is the HOPE = Help Others, Pain Ends.

When we see that the enemy is not someone else, but just another me then there is no fear of losing nor cheer of winning any more . . . . true victory is arriving at our own door. True Love has no fear . . . because there is no other . . . Me is the world and world is Me. Let us Converse with Universe.

"The weak can never forgive. Forgiveness is the attribute of the strong . . ."—Mahatma Gandhi

Vicious Cycle to Virtuous Cycle (*A thought by Mr. R.B. Sahi*)**:** When we closely observe lighting up an *agarbatti* (Incense Stick) in a slight breezy condition, we get a profound lesson. Now the giver (of fire) is the matchstick and the taker is the *agarbatti*. However, you will observe that the ability of the matchstick to keep burning increases radically, when it is in the process of lighting the *agarbatti*. Even though *agarbatti* is barely lit, there are moments when the breeze blows out the matchstick, but the *agarbatti* ignites the gaseous fumes that are coming from the matchstick and the match maintains its fire. The lessons:

○ First, the taker is as important as the giver. The world says the giver is noble—but the fact is that the taker is also noble. The taker enables the giver to be the giver. The giver grows when he gives. In fact the giver never gives—what is his to give?—He gets because the taker has to be given. What the giver has belongs to the taker. If the giver does not give, the taker will get it from someone else, and the one who has refused to give, will suffer. What he has hoarded will become toxic. As he gives, he creates space for more to come. The nature realizes that he is an efficient channel to reach out to the takers. The nature widens the range of stuff that flows to the giver. The fastest way of receiving is giving, but how do you give? You need takers. So be grateful to the takers—for they are the ones who enable you to grow. This has implications for the world economic order—for the importance of the third world and how it helps to maintain the health of the first world.

○ Second lesson is that what you thought was the taker, may have many things to give you. It may not be obvious to you—because you are blinded by what you have—so you have no respect for what he has. Be sure that he has what you need. You may not realize what you need. Actually, in abundance, all that you cognize is what you want and not what you need. So before you start respecting what the taker has that you need, you need to transcend the ego of abundance. The moment you do that, you will see the need and appreciate what the taker has. This can be done scientifically—all that you need to do is to face the breeze, which has the potential of extinguishing you. Then you will respect the *agarbatti*.

In practical terms, it means taking up challenges that stretch you—stretching is not only about remaining flexible—it is about creating space for growth to take place. The moment you stop growing, you are shrinking—you are dying. Therefore, the size of the challenge that you pick needs to be compatible with your stretch limits. Then you will know that you need something, and that something will come from unexpected corners—from those whom you never realized had anything to give. It will make you humble—it will make you ready to receive.

What could be a better challenge than to decide to give what you do not have? Such challenges initiate the virtuous cycle—enable the taker to get the joy of giving. You will not be able to feel grateful unless you value that which is given to you. Therefore, there is merit in remaining poor. Poor, with regard to what you need. The moment you have enough, increase your 'needs'—which is not to be confused with your 'wants', on the 'giver-taker-giver' paradigm and its potential for creating a virtuous cycle. (*End of thought.*)

It is said that there is chaos in the world, because, we instead of loving people and using things are doing the opposite, that is, using people and loving things. I feel, the idea of using by itself is chaotic, because the one who is habituated to use will use everything i.e. things as well as people, while the one who is used to loving will love everything, be it people or things. A soulful sms is far better than a mechanical hug.

Habitat reflects habit. Many have habit of craving and crying and few have the habit of helping and hugging. Let us have the habit of helping and hugging and be the true habitat of life . . .

Good Morning Tonic

- Relationship is Relay-tionship i.e. to win the race of life we have to have win-win relationship and it is like running a relay race where we inspire, ignite and integrate each other to achieve the goal
- To expect is a barrier, to accept is a carrier.
- *When we abandon Ego once, Love will overflow in abundance. When we Exit Ego, We exist as Eco and feel Love is an Eternal Echo.*
- We realise Existence neither loves nor hates but it is an echo. Be careful of Ego because whatever we throw will grow.
- HOPE = Help Others, Pain Ends
- An Angle where ego leaves and love lives makes you an Angel

Space to write your own tonic

What can beat me when I
experience that there is only one
beat that beats in every bit.

By Kiran Kurwade

9

Tonic for Great Team

Whenever we hear the word team, we think of a group of people. I feel, the basic teamwork is within us i.e. mind, heart, soul and body. If I am divided inside, I will be divided outside. If I am integrated inside, I can integrate with anybody and anything outside . . .

There lived two beggars; one was lame and the other blind. One day the hut where they lived caught fire, and they had to save themselves. What would they have done . . . any guesses? Yes, the lame man sat on the blind man's back and gave him directions, the blind ran fast carrying the lame and saved both of them.

Within self, there is always a conflict, and such conflicts are evident within departments, organizations and nations as well. It is Visionary vs. Task Master. The lame man had great vision but lacked technology; the blind man lacked spiritual vision but possessed technology. The tonic lies in striking the right balance between these two extremes, and in fact, communion of two into ONE is the need of an hour. We have to understand the Inter-dependence, the synergy . . . the TEAM SPIRIT.

Greater the balance we strike, greater the balance we create. Be the bank balance or work-life balance.

At night, we sometimes cannot sleep because there is a conflict between mind and heart. The one whose mind, heart, soul and body are united and integrated will experience bliss.

Teamwork gives great synergy. It is not 2+2=4 but can be 2+2=5 or more or sometimes less. Let us take an example of musical orchestra, which has many artists . . . the singer, the tabla player, the guitarist, the violinist, the drummer, etc. they all together create orchestra. Each one is unique and different from the other but when they come together with profound silence i.e. love, they form a divine harmony and great music manifests. They respect each other's uniqueness and hence synergize. If the flute player thinks he is the only musician and the drummer only creates noise, then he is wrong and he will not be able to co-create music. *If you are in sync, then you cannot sink.*

The previous chapter "Tonic for great Relationship", will be surely very relevant and helpful, especially the GLASS i.e. Gender-Looks-Show Off-Status. At workplace, there is a tendency of mis-judging people and being mis-led. There is cutthroat competition and the teamwork looks good in either books or some soft skills training programs. Team is moving from Me to We. Management studies have described it through various stages like **Forming, Storming, Norming, Performing and Closing.** Each stage is vital and it is an on-going phenomenon, it is either a new organization or a start-up.

Management can be a fun and a kind of SPORT: It is said that if a manager says he is a busy manager and often runs short of fulfilling his own KRA/KPI (key result areas/key performance indicators) then he is not an effective manager. In other words, he is a victim of an inability to manage time. In a fast-paced world, invariably one struggles to manage well. What is management? In the word itself the answer lies. It is manage men t i.e. 'manage' 'men' for 't' and 't' stands for Target, Task in given Time. I thought of SPORT and feel that Management Skills can broadly be put as SPORT, which is an acronym of Self, People, Opportunities, Resources & Tasks viz. managing Self, managing People, managing Opportunities, managing Resources and managing Time, Tasks & Targets.

Make it Easy, Enjoyable and Earning oriented: Let us take an example, the health freaks are often seen out there on the jogging tracks, going to gyms, performing yoga, meditation, etc. I wonder whether people really enjoy getting up early in the morning from their cosy beds and enjoy the workouts. If they get a hypothetical formula, say, just chant every day 6 times "I have 6 packs" and within 6 days they get 6 packs then how many of us will still go out in the field and work out? I think almost none of us will.

The children who get up early in the morning and study hard in fact also like to sleep a little more, but they make the effort to get up early and study in order to secure good marks. The habit works.

Human behaviour is mysterious; it is observed that prisoners who spend lifetime in jails clad in iron shackles become conditioned to such living conditions. When freed from their fetters, they often came back and request to be allowed living within jails, where they are comfortable with their shackles, in the dark and dingy rooms. The open space and sunlight is painful for them. They have become Happy Slaves. Can slavery be happy living? We have to be Awake, Arise and Achieve the truest form. Any work when done without passion seems hard work (busy), but when done with passion in the heart becomes easy.

Great teaming includes just intra and inter-personal teaming but also with material and machines. We often get irritated with our laptops and phones when they become slow or hang up. We have to feel them, heal them and grateful to them because they connect us to the world and materialize our objectives.

When we think we are Solo then we feel So Low, when we think we all are One then we have Won

Good Morning Tonic

- *Greater the balance we strike, greater the balance we create. Be the bank balance or work-life balance.*
- *What can beat me when i experience that there is only one beat that beats in every bit.*
- *Wave becomes the Way, Path becomes Play, When we drop our ego away*

- *If you are in sync then you cannot sink.*
- *A honey bee was asked, 'People crush your hive and rob your honey . . . it does not hurt you?" Bee said, "No, because they can take away my honey but can't take away my art of making honey" Source: Unknown*

Space to write your own tonic

Every father tries best to enable his child to achieve the greatness of life that he somehow missed to achieve. If every leader, be it a teacher or corporate manager can have such attitude for his people then humanity will evolve in leaps and bounds.

By Kiran Kurwade

10

Tonic for a Great Leader

Great Leadership is not about 'I am Power' but 'Empower'

When there is no difference between what we preach and what we practice then we make the difference.

Leader is Ladder: I often hear the word leader as ladder. In Leader, if we remove 'e' of Ego, and add 'd' of Develop . . . . it becomes Ladder. To most of us, leadership means leading from front, having followers, setting examples and winning accolades etc. I wonder then how many of such leaders truly enable their followers to go ahead of him/her and achieve much higher goals then he/she has accomplished?

Many times in pursuit of being a hero, one becomes like a banyan tree, so dominant that no other tree can grow underneath it or along with it. How many heroes can help to create other heroes?

We know Maslow's wonderful theory, where the first rung of ladder/pyramid is physiological need and at the top is Self-Actualization. True Leader is becoming an inspiring Ladder, which people climb for success. It is a quest for all leaders . . . . how many leaders have you created? How many can replace you? The myth is that many leaders often tend to create their own carbon copies, in reality one should enable others to flower in their own way. Rose is rose, Lotus is lotus and marigold is marigold . . . . it is foolishness if a rose tries to become a lotus . . . it cannot. The point is 'flowering' to the fullest. This is not merely a matter of philosophical studies, but is the basic of management studies called Succession Planning. A true leader is the one whose absence should not affect the team and work should go on smoothly. This reflects his style of being a Facilitative/ Coaching Leader. Likewise, there are many famous leadership styles: dictator, democratic, servant, situational etc., which is your style of leadership? Utilizing a right person for the right job at a right time is right leadership.

It is said, *"Efficient Leaders engage people with Mind, Effective engage with Heart and Great engage with Soul"*

Only cool headed can head ahead . . .

Are you a Great Leader? At workplaces, a leader has his team and a leader above him, especially when we think of any organization. It is a common practice and the team leaders say that if they receive pressure they will give pressure, i.e. if they hear abusive language from their seniors they magnify and use the same down the line. Somewhere someone has to end this. Can a leader be a shock absorber i.e. absorb the negative part and percolate the positive part down to the team so that the team doesn't get de-motivated and achieves the mission.

We cannot generalize a formula of managing people, as not all five fingers are same, so are people. As rightly said, people do not leave an organization, but they leave their bosses. Owing to this, often an organization suffers from very high attrition. Word of mouth publicity makes it an unwanted organization to work with; eventually the organization loses its credibility in the market and faces serious adverse effects on its business in the end.

There is a great leadership lesson to be learnt from **Lord Shiva** in Hindu mythology. During **"Samudra Manthan"** when the poison came out, the question was who will save the earth from it. It was Shiva who had great compassion towards everybody and was ready to bear the pain of drinking the poison, BUT significantly had an amazing ability to digest the poison and remain unaffected thereafter.

Similarly, a true leader cares for his each team player, doesn't handle things emotionally and invite dangerous and unwanted problems for himself, his team, or organization; rather increases the capacity of self and entire team to face any tough situation and win harmoniously. Building capacity is about continuous learning and development, and upgrading with modern technology, tools and techniques.

4R Approach—Respect (R1), Reward (R2), Reprimand (R3) and Retrench (R4)

As we learned, it is meaningless to generalize a formula to deal with various people because each one has different value system thus different motivating factors and different approaches work for different people. *Many people, many retinas (visions & values).* However, we can think of an order/sequence/process. Foremost is a Respect for people, which actually means to consider everyone equal i.e. no superior and no inferior. Nowadays, few leaders practice it and these leaders would be essentially the great leaders. It works miraculously provided we think long term and have abundance of patience, passion and perseverance. It reflects 'Divinity Intelligence' refer to 4D Intelligence in chapter 'Tonic for great Intelligence'. May I quote *Maryada Purushottam Ram* as **RAM i.e. Right Attitude Man hence Right Action Man**. During his reign, the mankind witnessed great justice, great prosperity and great peace because he instilled great humility = great humanity. He was so powerful and yet so humble.

Respect is timeless, everyone want respect. Today earning **Money** is not much a problem but **Money + Respect** together is rare. It is quite evident in today's life where people have multiple options of career/job and expect a respectful treatment from the bosses and management.

Unfortunately, most of the organizations and leaders due to heavy pressure, quick-fix approach and lack of time tend to follow only, which is not good for any organization. In such cases, the performers and sensitive people leave the organization and organizations face not just high attrition rate but lose the quality people, the cost in recruitment and training and the trust in the market.

Second is Reward. People love to be recognized and hence organizations are always on their toes to plan and practice various remunerative and non-remunerative employee engagement programs. Reward and Reprimand go hand in hand i.e. Carrot and Stick. Lastly, when we have tried everything but still we do not get desired results than the final resort would be to Retrench which is painful to an employee as well as the employer. Unfortunately, most of us practice Reward, Reprimand and Retrench because it is easy to find other others mistakes and hardly practice Respect, which is mirroring Self. Mostly and sadly, the retrenchment happens at front end employees. If at all, the retrenchment then it should begin with retrenching the team leaders who were responsible for the poor show or unable to motivate and educate people down the line. The 4R approach has been derived from *Sam-Dam-Dand-Bhed philosophy as practiced by great guru Chanakya.*

Hero Vs. Hero: Who is a Hero? I feel HERO stands for being Highly Ethical, Result Oriented. It is often said win the race either by any means, but in long terms it has been observed that only Ethics, Enlightenment and Empowerment sustain. Because we can fool, some people for some time but not all the people all the time and significantly how can one fool oneself. Is it a war between the hero and a villain? No, it is between, hero versus hero. We experience this in our day-to-day personal and professional lives. In any debate, the other is also true. The ignorant thinks only he is right and others are wrong. He lacks the holistic vision. Say, two people standing opposite each other looking through a bent wall of transparent glass . . . the glass is concave for one and the convex for the other . . . both see the world through their dented and distorted vision, and interpret accordingly. The solution is empathizing or exchanging positions and looking through, then realizing the other can also be also true. A great leader views every one as equal. There is no barrier between him and the others. According to him, if he is a hero then everybody is a potential hero. *If we can DERIVE Love from everything in Life, then we can lovingly DRIVE anything in Life . . .*

On contrary we say am a hero and the other is a zero. It is about Winning or to Defeating, and if one is focused on winning, he wins self and others also, while if one is focused on defeating others, he gets defeated by self and others also.

Sometimes some words and concepts are misleading like Leadership. Conventionally it means to lead, and in this pursuit, the person often turns individualistic. He tries always to be different and superior to others to win accolades. He becomes an index finger giving instructions, a great leader should be like a humble thumb, which can join with all the fingers and form a multi-purpose hand, and if required a powerful fist.

"Leadership is doing what is right when no one is watching . . ."—George Van Valkenburg

How much is too much? *(A thought by Mr. R.B. Sahi)* Take a bottle, full of water and try emptying it. You will find that the maximum rate of flow is achieved when you provide a little opening for air to come in. In other words, something counterintuitive happens, i.e. tilting the bottle all the way, creates considerable commotion in the water, but the flow achieved is less. This has two lessons:

- First, if you are fanatical about anything, a perfectionist/ a purist, who does not permit any reverse movement, however small it is, w and makes absolute statements like—I always—, I never—etc., then most likely he will be false, a fraud and a short lived entity. It is when you permit opposition to exist that will help you to prolong your life. If you permit Bacteria, you will gain immunity. If you permit criticism, you will be effective.
- Second lesson is to practice moderation in everything, i.e. put in efforts, but not to the point where everything else is excluded. There is a right amount of effort (tilt), beyond which the effort becomes toxic. It creates very severe side effects—even though you are making a statement—proving to yourself that you are fully committed—you are in fact destroying whatever you are trying to create. Therefore, live a life of moderation, where you must be effective as well as relaxed. (End of thought).

Valuables vs. Values: I also feel it is not valuables but values, which we should leave for generations to come. Would it not be then a true legacy, because after many years it will hardly matter what car we drove today, the house we lived in or the bank balance we had, **but** how many children we inspired with love and peace. It is only love and peace, which integrates the world.

Great Leader gives Positive responses to Negative situations

Good Morning Tonic

- *Lord Ram has been a great inspiration since my childhood, I derive the learning from the very name RAM as Right Attitude Man, hence a Right Action Man*
- *Leader cannot Lead without Legwork,*
  Team cannot Triumph without Teamwork,
  Happiness cannot happen without hard work (heart work)
- *The decision taken without any Fear and Favour brings out our best Flavour.*
- *If life is an examination, then being an inspiring example others, is passing it with flying colours.*
- *The one who fights against fire and extinguishes it becomes the hero in people's eyes, but the real hero is the one who prevents the fire anonymously.*

Space to write your own tonic

Until we have any EXCUSE to FAIL,
we can't USE our greatest
strength to SAIL.

By Kiran Kurwade

11

Tonic for Great Professional

Higher the Interest (passion), Higher the Interest (profit)

*Higher the **Reason** (Goal), Higher the **Reach,** hence higher the **Results** achieved.*

What is Ownership? There lived two young men called Raju & Sanju in a small village. 15 KMs from their village an organization had set up a factory of consumer durables and the two men joined the factory as office boys. One day the weather was bad, and it started raining heavily as they were returning home. Suddenly, Sanju said "*Oh I forgot to switch off one of the lights in the office*". On hearing this Raju said "*So what . . . switch it off tomorrow morning and nobody will ever know because it we who reach office before anyone else does and leave only after all have left.*" Sanju did not listen to him, and went back to office despite the bad weather and switched off the light.

After 15 years later, they the two friends met each other at a market place in the same village. Sanju got out of his big car to meet his friend. They were happy to see each other after so many years. While talking Raju came to know that Sanju was doing very well. He said to Sanju, "Hey buddy, it seems you have become a great man" and asked, "*Have you become an **owner** of some company?*

Sanju responded assertively, "*Owner?, I was an owner even 15 years back. So what if I was just an office boy, I always worked there thinking it was my own company. If you remember, I had gone to switch off the lights because I did not want to see my company incurring any damage or losses. This very quality of ownership I inculcated in me and any organization I worked with I gave them my 100%. Today I am growing happily. I am placed in a good position and receive good salary but my biggest achievement is a sense of satisfaction and peace of mind"*

This is ownership, a basic acumen of being a great Professional. Ownership is about giving 100% to a company. Often we think in terms of what the company, society or nation has given us, instead we should rather question ourselves, *"What I have given them?"*

What is the meaning of Professional? When we observe the word Profit . . . . we see it's made by the one who is Professionally Fit. **PROFIT** = **PRO**fessionally **FIT**

So, who is a Professional? The word 'profess' is related to the oath-taking procedures followed by any religious order. We know the oath taking process of various professionals, like soldiers, politicians, or witnesses in the court. However, the question here is, how many truly follow their oath/promise?

Sometimes promise may not give immediate profit but we know there are few things, which are beyond profit and loss, and in long run they will surely give prosperity i.e. right profit.

The one who strikes the balance will have great balance be it bank balance or work-life balance.

Another confusing aspect is whether the person is different at professional and personal fronts? Example, if we have a fight at home in the morning, doesn't it show at office and vice-versa? Hence, the division becomes confusion, and blind analysis leads to paralysis. What is the way out of this?

Cinema gives us a good lesson in this regard . . . a great actor is one who is easily de-conditioned from any character he plays, therefore allowing him to play any given role, even multiple roles at the same time. Since he is not conditioned to any role, he can take up any role and give 100% justice to the given role.

Therefore, it is about fulfilling all our roles and responsibilities honestly, as a human being, a citizen, a son, a father, a boss, a subordinate, a salesman, or a customer. A police officer cannot favour his son who has been found involved in criminal activities; he must treat his son (a criminal) the way he treats other criminals.

It is not between person to person BUT Problem (Dark) to Solution (Light). **Attack the Problem not the Person, Appreciate the Principle not the Person.** An awakened person is like a Sun who spreads its light equally.

I would like to share the learning from Coconut, which has mythological significance in India and are being offered to the Gods. Coconut also has great utilitarian values, like its water, milk, oil, coir etc.

It is easy to pierce into an unripe coconut, since the shell and the fruit are attached to each other closely. However, in case of a ripe, matured coconut, especially the dried one (copra), it is difficult to touch the fruit. The fruit inside is very strong and has detached from the shell.

The immature professionals are like unripe coconut. They easily get bogged down with external pressure; for instance ruthless treatment from people, clever trade, changing market, cutthroat competition, etc. They are vulnerable and can be easily broken into pieces. Matured professionals remain detached, under any kind of pressure and continue to give their best, like the dried coconut fruit that gives rich oil.

When I contemplate on our great leaders from varying lifestyles, I sense they are like matured coconuts. Powerful from within, they remain detached from sorrow and ups & downs in life, non-fluctuating in their FOCUS, taking wise decisions and create Revolution. Nothing can beat them . . . . that is why Mahatma Gandhi could say, "*They may torture my body, break my bones or even kill me. They will have my body, not my obedience*". Because his soul was de-conditioned from the body . . . he was a master and not a slave to his body (external world).

"The true profession of man is to find his way to himself . . ."
—Hermann Hesse

3Ps—People, Planet & Profit: It is the moral responsibility of professionals, especially every business professionals not to focus on profit alone. Short sightedness makes few business groups call it a smart strategy where they aim at earning profit by any means. A great businessperson respects **People**, all stakeholders, internal as well as external customers. He earnestly works for the development of his people because it is the people who make or break an organization. Significantly, he works on taking care of the **Planet** i.e. mother Earth. He will not produce or manufacture any product that can deteriorate the environment, or disturb the ecological balance. The word profit can thus be replaced by **Prosperity**, as it is not related merely to financial aspects, but all other aspects that turn the world into a **Peaceful** living place.

Avenue to Revenue: The Venue when prefixed with A of Aspiration it becomes Avenue, and when it is prefixed with Re of Results, it becomes Revenue.

The point is being a profit (prosperous) centre. Every organization, every department, every branch, every individual is a profit centre. *A Gain is when we get Again and Again . . . noble and new.*

Answer lies in the Market: One of the disciples of Buddha held a butterfly in his hand and asked Buddha, "Tell me if the butterfly is alive or dead?" He was thinking that if Buddha responds "alive" then he will crush it to death, and if Buddha responds "dead" then he will let it go "alive," just to prove Buddha wrong. Buddha replied, "The answer lies in your hands"

So is the answer in business management. Business leaders have always said, *"The answer lies in the market"*. How much do you understand the nerves of the market? Various customers, geographies, cultures, expectations, competitors, challenges, various product range of our products . . . opportunities. It is the customer who tells us what he wants, and that is precisely what drives business growth.

Greater the Network, Greater the Net worth

If I have a food, then I am also a food.

By Kiran Kurwade

Good Morning Tonic

- *To establish oneself as good, we demolish the real good and thus turn the world and ourselves into just the goods.*
- *Tragedy of Human Race is that it has turned into a Rat Race, We often find an Evil Trace behind the so-called Good Face.*
- *Humanity can take a great Turn if we do good without expecting anything in Return.*
- *It does not matter what path you walk . . . what matters is how FAIR you act and how FAR you walk.*

Space to write your own tonic

A mediocre teacher says, "My job is to take the horse near water but if the horse doesn't drink then it's not my fault." But a great teacher says "My job is not just to take the horse near water but ensure the journey is so inspiring & insightful that the horse has to drink water and if it doesn't then somewhere i failed in my job"

by Kiran Kurwade

12

Tonic for a Great Change Maker

'B' Positive may or may not be everyone's blood group, but from womb to tomb, it runs in all of us and can change us from Idle to Ideal . . .

Am I honest with the person in the Mirror? A mediocre teacher says, *"My job is to take the horse near the water, but if the horse doesn't drink then it's not my fault."* However, a great teacher says, *"My job is not just to take the horse near the water but to ensure the journey is so inspiring and insightful that the horse would willingly drink water and if it doesn't, then somewhere i have failed in my job . . ."* Isn't he a great Change Maker?

Such is a self-motivated approach of every honest professional in his or her respective field. For example, a great salesperson will echo the same feeling about customers. If the customers are not buying his company products then he will think that he has failed somewhere in his efforts. A true team leader would express similar sentiments about his team players. From time to time, the processes and systems have to be re-visited if they are to me made relevant to the current context, or they will become obsolete. Systems are made for people; people are not made for system.

"Everyone thinks of changing the world but no one thinks of changing self" **Leo Tolstoy**

Are we sowing the Right Seeds? If we retrospect and introspect the way we raise our children, we find that when a one-year-old child starts walking, he falls down many times, hits things around him, like tables, chairs, etc., and starts crying. What we do to make him stop crying? We hit that table or chair, and say that it has caused the child pain, so it should be taught a lesson. We do it in a funny way, because we want the child to stop crying and start laughing. Are we not sowing the seeds of violence and revenge in a young life? Seeds of a life full of hatred and do this how things should work? We impose our own beliefs and dreams on our children and thus shut the doors for him to self-explore. No wonder, he grows up as a confused person. His confusion and misery increase as he grows up and starts going in school, and college, and later in life takes up some profession. We may speak of very high principles, but how we behave and act plays a vital role. A father may counsel a child that anger is very bad, but if he says that angrily, and shouts *"How many times should I tell you that anger is bad?"* now, what could be more confusing for a child? When we get sick or get injured, we repeatedly say "I am sick, I am sick, I am sick" without realizing that we are magnifying it in the mind of child. He becomes susceptible to negativity and becomes weaker and weaker. Entire water of sea cannot drown the ship but just a small hole can.

Have we chosen Life or Life has chosen us? We know the story of the rebirth of an Eagle. It goes through a painful process of change when it gets older in life. Eagle initiates a change; it plucks out its feathers, claws, and beak and is re-born as a winning eagle again. The upbringing of eagle is also challenging, the mother gives a dangerous push to its eaglets from a great height . . . experiencing danger, the eaglets emerge out as winner. Eagle gives us many lessons . . . . when it rains all the birds take refuge in trees, etc. but it is only an eagle who dares to fly above the clouds, i.e. *Problems, Pressure and Pain*. The spirit of the eagle lurks within all of us. May I say that **E.A.G.L.E = Excel Above Given Level Every time**

EAGLE stands for Excel Above Given Level Everytime.

By Kiran Kurwade

We all know that change is the only constant thing in the world. A **learning aspirant must explore what are the causes of Change. What are the degrees of Change? Does change occur very fast or dead slow or is there something, which is beyond change?** For instance—when we make knots in a handkerchief, it undergoes changes but the fabric remains same.

Planets move in fixed orbits/trajectories. Mercury cannot jump into the orbit of Venus and start revolving there. From the Earth, the Sun will appear to rise only from the East and this will remain unchanged. And if it changes then it could be the annihilation day. In addition, there is something, which is changing so fast that human eyes cannot perceive, like the dynamic changes on the sun being at the fourth state of matter Plasma.

In the context of Business Management, what is not changing and what is changing too fast? Desiring a profit has not changed; right from the ancient times, anybody who wanted to do business of any kind, expected some kind of a gain. The marketing strategies may however change from time to time, place to place and person to person. Customer expectations are changing rapidly with the wide scale growth in technology. He can travel to any part of world, come back and compare the products and services. Moreover, even if does not travel, he watches it on television. The biggest challenge for the business organizations is to anticipate the change and exceed the expectations of customers.

Is there something, which does not Change? If everything changes then how one could experience or exchange the changes? Some point in the experiencer has to be beyond change. Eyes do not see the light but even in the darkness, one cannot make out what is dark and what is light. It is not always being positive . . . there is something which is above positive and negative. What is that? Whatever we call it . . . the point is everything can be questioned, except that 'point' which experiences everything.

Be the Centre. Have you wondered why the Target of the dart or any shooting game is to hit at the Centre? *Because the Purpose, Promise & Passion should not change.* Hence, practices like customer service are coined as Customer Centric because he is the centre; according to his requirement all policies, processes and people are strategized. They are the reason behind the existence of all business organisations.

The centre of atom, i.e. nucleus, around which electrons, protons, and neutrons revolve, is similar to the centre of the solar system called Sun, around which planets revolve. Being at the periphery is being idle, dependent BUT Being the centre is being powerful . . . the pull . . . the ideal. Be the centre and make your brand the centre.

The wheel moves, but not the axle. The axle holds the wheel but it has to be free from the wheel and well-lubricated, etc. If it gets jammed with the wheel then the vehicle meets with an accident. When we become the centre, work becomes worship; it turns from stressful to soulful, effortful to effortless, complicated to simple. It does not mean one becomes complacent, but utterly committed and hence more competent. **Be the Centre . . . Be Conscious, Be the Controller, Be a Conqueror.**

I can see the change because there is something in me, which is beyond change. Those who just talk, they call it fate. Those who walk the talk, they call it faith. When we begin to hear faith for fate, the universe opens it gate.

Who can Change? The being that aspires to become 'that,' which he does not want to change, and resists change. The successful and well-established people often resist change because they do not want to invite the risk of losing their current success. Is it that people change only when there are multiple options or they change when there is no option? Does a crisis point become the rising point?

It is said that if weekdays do not excite you then change your job, if weekends do not excite you then change your friends. I feel if neither job nor friends excite you then you have to change yourself.

Choosing a Positive Change is a Great Change: How does an Oyster gives birth to a Pearl? When a foreign element slips between the mantle and shell of an Oyster, it causes unbearable pain t the creature within it. It is so inspiring to know that the Oyster then produces enough layers of nacre and over the years, the irritating object is converted into a Pearl. The Irritant is converted into Stimulant, the Pain into Pearl. Isn't it a great ability? Such is the Attitude, Approach & Action of a great Change Maker. He performs best under pressure. In fact, the performance under pressure is 'the best performance,' be it in personal or professional life, and inspires others to adopt changes. It is said, "*Give me a serenity to accept that I cannot change courage to change that which I can change and the wisdom to know the difference between the two . . .*"

Idle to Ideal: Most of us must have a heard a story of a father, son and the starfishes. One early morning a father and his five-year-old son went to seashore. The father sat on the rock and after sometime sees his son dancing on the beach. When he moved closer, he was surprised to see his son gathering starfishes in his little hands and throwing them back into the sea. The starfishes that were brought in by the waves were dying. Father said to his son, "You are being stupid . . . you are wasting your efforts because there are thousands of fishes dying . . . . how many will you save? What difference does it makes?" The son with a twinkle in his eyes aid, "Father . . . . I don't know what difference it makes, but surely it'll make a difference to these two dying fishes, when I'll throw them back into the water . . ." Even in social services, we opt to work for many people and get fame or do not work at all; whereas the little boy was a true change maker. However, some performances cannot be valued or measured because the tools of measurement fall too short; the importance is felt after many years.

It is said, "*Giving fish will not work we have to teach people fishing.*"

Let us Share to increase the Share: Imagine a room in where there are 100 candles, which are not lit up, hence the room looks dark. Visualize the candles are alive. One candle wakes up and gets lit, but if she is cynical and thinks that she will not enlighten the others sleeping, because it's her USP of being the only enlightened one, then there would be no difference between her and the others, and her importance would be lost and the room will have limited brilliance. HOWEVER, if this candle becomes compassionate and enlightens all the other candles then visualize the brilliance of the room. Irrespective of the size of the candle, the brightness is the same, so it is not the position but our ability to spread light that matters. Practically, in the process of enlightening others nothing of the candle is lost, even its age remains unaffected. When all the candles are enlightened then the 'collective brilliance' will **co-create** abundance of Light, of love, peace & prosperity towards team, organization, nation and our world and we shall co-evolve.

"The life lived for others is the only life to be worthwhile . . ."
Einstein

I get inspirations from every Buddha, i.e. the one who is awakened and awakens others, or we can say anyone who changes himself and enables change for others, be it a social or business entrepreneur. One of my favourite Change Makers of all times is Samrat Ashoka, who changed from Chand (Cruel) Ashok to Buddha Ashok i.e. Ashoka the Great

When we GET the Truth,
we become a GATE of Truth.

By Kiran Kurwade

Good Morning Tonic

- The only FORM that is permanent is TRANSFORM
- Unless man does not become Kind, how can we call it as Mankind?
- *When we are with the FLOW of nature, we become a FLOWer of nature*
- *There is no Grave worse than being a happy Slave,*
  A Crisis Point becomes a Rising Point for the Brave.

- *Wake & Walk is same . . . those who wake up will walk down to wake up others . . .*
- *It does not matter how many people you change, what actually matters is have you changed yourself.*

Space to write your own tonic

13

Tonic by Great Mother

Are we caring enough our mother when she gets old and needs us the most?

In a race for earning money, we often tend to move far away from our mother. The 'M' of Mommy is hijacked by 'M' of Money and the Mother looks just like Other. HOWEVER, for our mothers we never become Others. She is the only person who loves us at all times. Religions say that if heaven exists then it is under the mother's feet. Mother does not love; she personifies the very word LOVE.

Why is it that a mother is capable of sensing the difficulties that her children are going through, even though they may live far way? This is because she is spiritually connected to her children, and physiologically connected through the placenta. The connections are deep and strong.

There are many great lessons to be learnt from a mother: When we ask for food, we always get something. She may starve, but ensures that here children are fed and happy. She is a great manager, and functions beyond all management practices . . . be it Crisis Management, People Management, Time Management, Stress Management, Service management. Her very touch is healing.

Motherhood is Creativity and Care of People, Projects & Processes with divine passion and indomitable willpower. The feminine form is divine energy that is Serene, Soft and Synergizing. Women at work exhibit a blend of Maturity, Motherliness and Magnetism, thus have greater Managerial abilities.

Today's modern manager has to be more motherly, else he/she will fail to conquer challenges like attrition, grievances, teamwork, patience, resilience, co-evolution, which are the success pillars of brand equity.

A mother is an embodiment of "Ownership" she does not disown the child, rather enables the child to highlight his/her potential to the highest level. We come across many projects/mission in our personal or professional lives, and we see it is easy to proclaim oneself as the father of any successful project/mission, but hardly anyone digests failure of the project/mission, and takes complete ownership to revive it, that is being the Mother. Because mother does not expect any credit, rather selflessly enables growth of the child, especially when the child (mission) is in great Difficulty, Disgraced and Dishonoured.

One day a busy manager on his weekly off takes his old mother for a shopping along with the family. While the wife and children were shopping, the man gets some time to spend with his mother. Mother insists to go to an old place, which she used to visit when he was a small child. Therefore, mother and son visit the nostalgic place, a place where many birds come and people feed them with grains.

They sit for some time and the mother asks the son about a bird, "Which bird is this? Son replies "Wild pigeon". Mother asks again and son gives the same reply, the mother repeats the question and this time the son gets angry and says, "I told you, its wild pigeon, don't you understand?" Mother replies with a heavy voice, "Son, when you were young, you had asked this question many times and every time I had kissed your forehead and replied lovingly"

If at all the world exists amid so much of chaos, it is only because of loving beings and true love is instilled, illuminated & inspired by a mother.

Thank you Mother!

Space to write your own tonic

When we view the Truth of Inner world, we shall have a Real view of Outer world.

By Kiran Kurwade

Good Morning Tonic

Kiran Kurwade has shared his self-conceived insights in the form of 1 or 2 liners, which you might have imbibed in almost every page of this book, sharing separately some of it. You may find interesting and would like to share as Good Morning Tonic with your near and dear ones on phone, Facebook or Twitter etc.

- When a mind is free from every "ism" it becomes a pure prism
- Great Leadership is not about "I am Power" but "Empower"
- Belief is an evolutionary seed that can grow into revolutionary Leaf provided we remove the weed of disbelief . . .
- The great NEWS of Life is that it is always NEW when we see it with our Soul
- SOUL stands for Spirit Of Universal Love
- HOPE=Help Others, Pain Ends
- FEE of Success = Faith, Explore, Excel
- GIFT= God is Freedom and Truth
- When I am 'Asleep' dreams seem real, when I am 'Awake' reality seems like a dream
- As we Believe so we Live
- Every Stone can be a Milestone
- If we can DERIVE Love from everything in Life, then we can Lovingly DRIVE anything in Life . . . .
- Humanity can take a great Turn if we do good without expecting anything in Return
- Black & White are not opposite of each other but composite of each other.
- When Love calls, the Ego falls
- Live this moment as it is our last, because it will never last
- Meditation is not about renouncing the world,
- It is about bouncing back with Compassion for the world

- We have moved from Cart to Car, but remained far from each other's hearts.
- Only Love and Love alone can bring us closer.
- Leader cannot Lead without Legwork, Teamwork cannot Triumph without Teamwork, Happiness cannot Happen without Hard work (heart work)
- I feel . . . true freedom is not in becoming any flying form, but to become the very formless sky in which various forms fly . . .
- When we view the Truth of Inner world,
- We shall have a Real view of the Outer world!
- We are getting so busy with our Touch Screens, that we are forgetting the touch of Living Beings
- When we GET the Truth, we become a GATE of Truth
- When we are with the FLOW of nature,
- We become a FLOWer of nature!
- No Sin of yesterday can prevent me in becoming the Saint of today
- When you meet and embrace Love at life's every rung,
- You emit grace and remain always beautiful & young!
- I do not know if wish comes true from a shooting star, but I know if you truly wish love then you'll shine like a star
- The most glorious catwalk is when you walk the path of Love & Light.
- When there is no difference between what we preach and what we practice, then we can make a difference!
- When we bow to the colours of life, then we become the rainbow of life!
- When we see that the enemy is no other but just another me, then there is no fear of losing or cheer of winning. True Love has no fear, because there is no other, me is the world and world is me.
- The nature of matter is to revolve and that of non-matter is to evolve
- Illusion= Ill+Vision
- Enemy is just Another Me
- Happiness is like a horizon, the more we go near the further it appears
- Every father wants his child to achieve the height of success that he himself has not achieved. If every leader, be it a teacher or corporate manager, has this attitude for his people then humanity will evolve in leaps and bounds

- Once we abandon the ego,
- Love will overflow in abundance . . . The more we become 'godown'(accumulate) the more we will go down
- An Angel is one who cannot Die, but without Love, she cannot Live nor Fly.
- To love it does not matter how long you Live, what matters is how well you get along, while you Live.
- True Lover is not a Lover who cannot Love Forever . . . it is Now or Never . . . .
- It is said Darkness is not opposite of Light, but the absence of Light. Moreover, it is quite right; however, can we go deeper and realize that there is no Darkness? It is our inability to see the Light everywhere and every time. In fact everything is Light . . . there is nothing but light. As for a true lover everything is filled with Love . . . there is no hatred but just Love.
- "Role with Goal is like Body with Soul . . ."
- It is imperative to move from SMART to SMARTER Goals . . .
- SMARTER = Specific, Measurable, Achievable, Realistic, Time Bound, Enjoyable & Rejuvenating
- When we feel Love at its root,
- Life becomes musical like a flute!
- When we give Love so much,
- Life becomes light like feather touch!
- Whenever I fight against the "Wrong" I become more "Strong"
- Let my body bend like wind, heart flow like water, eyes rain like cloud, mind be stable like a rock and the soul serene and 'witnessing' like the sky . . . .
- Heavier the Heart-Brake, Higher the Heart-Break
- If I can't Love one, I can't Love anyone and if I can Love one then I can Love anyone
- *Jise buddhi ke astitva ka bodh nahi wah buddhu,*
- *Aur jise astitva ke buddhi ka bodh ho wah Buddha.*
- When we start hearing "Unable" as "Enable", we become an Able in the true sense . . .
- Wake & Walk is same . . . those who wake up will walk down to wake up others . . .
- Solitude is Soul's Attitude & Solution is Soul's Salvation
- Whether we are Rich or Poor, the real joy of any Weather is when we are Together, Let's Gather Love Together

- The more I SLEEP in desire the more I SLIP into deadly fire . . .
- Whether we are Rich or Poor, a real joy of any Weather is when we are Together, so let's Gather Love Together
- The spirit required to tune up a mind and tone up the muscle, breathes within the heart, which can turn down any obstacle
- Leader is like a Ladder
- If I want to RELIEVE myself . . . then I have to RE-LIVE the unlived moments. When we mirror our memories then we become strong enough to heal . . .
- A mediocre teacher says, "My job is to take the horse near water but if the horse doesn't drink then it's not my fault." However, a great teacher says, "My job is not just to take the horse near water, but to ensure that the journey is so inspiring & insightful that the horse will willingly drink water, and if it doesn't then somewhere I have failed in my job . . ."
- We can READ . . . only when we are READY
- If the universe is infinite and life is eternal then there has to be infinite types of living beings . . .
- If we can make robots, then we can also b a kind of robot made by some other superior robots.
- They say the origin of life is water. Yes, I feel it is the water in eyes . . .
- Doesn't it reflect the truest of life, which is nothing but love?
- Space and Time is one: No Space, No Time.
- Infinite Space, Infinite Time.
- Let us widen our vision to see the infinite space and that is being truly in the Now
- When Truth is real-ised on the way,
- Then me, my and mine gets blown away
- When we Exit Ego, We exist as Eco, and feel Love is an Eternal Echo
- Tragedy of the Human Race is that it has turned into a Rat Race,
- We often find an Evil Trace behind the so called Good Face
- To establish oneself as good, we demolish the real good, thus making way for ourselves and the world to turn into mere goods
- Great Intellect is just not to deflect the outer Object, but to conquer inner defects and reflect positive Effects
- When we are bogged down in life then we often REMEMBER the most happiest/touching moments, and it gives us strength to knock down any barrier . . .

- Actually, we all are MEMBERS of a common and divine club called life. At times when we forget, just close the eyes, feel the vibes and we will RE-MEMBER again the truest aspect of life i.e. just Love. Love is the greatest power
- Once we Consciously Enter inside, we become a Centre without any side
- If a superfast train of big opportunities doesn't stop at our station then it doesn't mean it's not our train, but either we are at the wrong station or our station is too small for such trains
- Sky is the experiencer and anything that flies in it, the birds, the clouds, is the experience. No cloud can be bigger than the sky and the beauty of sky lies in the flying birds, clouds, stars, planets, Sun etc. The holistic perspective would be when the Sky (Experiencer) and Clouds(Experience) complement each other and become One
- When we play the MUSIC of Life, we create the MAGIC of Life!
- There is something which integrates us, it converts every cry into joy . . . it can never die and it is ONE therefore it is COMMON!
- It does not matter if its day or night,
- The point is do we have the ability to clearly see the light!
- Every bit is lit up, for those who have lit their inner self!
- If I have a food then I will be the food!
- Once you put your feet down, then nobody can defeat you because the real fight is not between you and others, but you and yourself!
- A Gain is when we get Again and Again!
- Black is nothing but Lack of Brilliance (Light)!
- If we turn our back and run away from Light, bigger shadow will follow us. Just return back to Light and we are home
- When the Sky gets tearful it rains, the Sun feels the pain and makes it smile in the form of a Rainbow. Be a Rainbow Smile in someone's Tears!
- As long as we see our usual face then we are stuck at the surface, Real fun starts when we face the faceless face!
- When it becomes our nature to keep rising after every fall, then our signature becomes an inspiring autograph for all!
- If you Wait for Light from others . . . it'll create an unbearable Weight,
- Let yourself breathe the Light . . . it'll permeate so deep that,
- You will become the Light and then your eyes will get Wet in gratitude!

- Steaming Performance is a result of Soulful Teaming!
- It is a Soulful Leader who instils a sense of great Esteem in a Team, which in turn helps to produce Steaming Performance . . . .
- The more we remain awake and walk the talk,
- The more life becomes a cake walk!
- The more we postpone life, the more we become alone in life!
- Heart pains until we are caged in the Mind's fence,
- See through Love's lenses, and sense Life's essence,
- It says . . . to Love and be Loved we do not need any license!
- Time melts when we melt into the Timelessness!
- There is no Grave worse than being a happy Slave,
- A Crisis Point becomes a Rising Point for the Brave!
- When a loving heart Paints the Pain,
- It can't get washed away by any Rain
- STILL Mind plays with a STEEL Body!
- Any decision taken without Fear and Favour brings out our best Flavour
- It does not matter what path you walk . . . what matters is how FAIR and FAR you walk . . .
- Knowledge is when Knowing becomes a Living Edge.
- It is a great responsibility, so use it judiciously at every Stage!
- Oh, God! Let me be . . .
  * So selfless that I don't ask anything for myself
  * So silent that I listen to every painful voice
  * So sensitive that I feel every unexpressed pain
  * So spacious that I take their pain in me
  * So serene that I live and die to heal them with right knowledge!

- If at all you wish to give me something, then give me the strength that I Walk the Talk of Love, Peace and Truth!
- The one who has won his self completely, can live in the now freely!
- If we cannot connect through our Eyes then we cannot connect through any Device!
- Is True Love about "To be Loved" or "To Love"?
- 'To be Loved' is the nature of body and 'To Love' is related to the soul, hence 'To be Loved' shall drop someday, but 'To Love' is ever enduring, endless and eternal!
- Conversion of Need into Want into Demand is Business, done via Sale,

- Conversion of Demand into Want into Need, is Easiness done via Soul!
- Honey bee collects nectar from flowers to make honey,
- Human being create war from power to make money,
- What can beat me when I experience that there is, only one beat that beats in every bit
- There is nothing to win and nothing to lose, when there is no-thing to choose!
- Heart and Hurt is One . . . without Eclipse there is no Sun
- Without Hurt the Heart has no meaning,
- Sun gives light, but at times wears the dark ring,
- Smiling lips also experience occasional sad eclipses!
- Te choice is not about Choosing a Rich or Poor Life but being ALIVE at every Life
- When I am able to observe the thought, I am able to absorb that thought.
- I can see the change because there is something in me which is beyond change
- The nature of mind is to think but the choice is in our hands to let it flow like water or let it sink like the sand. If we are with the flow then we grow, otherwise we get conditioned to a mind-set and become stagnant.
- Life can be known best when I am on my own and at rest,
- Before I ask for divinely help, my task is to totally unmask myself
- Higher we 'Arrange', higher we 'Range'
- Life is moving from Zero (Birth, ignorance) to Zero (Death, enlightenment . . . nothingness) in a Zero (Life-Cycle)
- Invisible does not mean not visible, but in-visible (visible inside).
- If life is an examination then being an inspiring example is passing it with flying colours
- Life is the greatest paradox . . . it is together one and many, universal and unique, particle and wave, body and soul, tears and smile, good and bad; in fact it is multi coloured, shades of one colour, rainbow from a single light.
- Right teaching is a motherly process, a journey of thought (knowledge) to taught(wisdom),conceiving, nurturing, delivering and setting it free
- Higher the Interest (passion),
- Higher the Interest (profit)

- Prayers are answered of those whose hearts are Pure, and the point is that such people will never pray for themselves!
- It is said that every person is born for some purpose. Does a person create a purpose or does a purpose create the person? Is it the dreamer who creates dreams or do the dreams create a dreamer? World is a fair and its fare is to give as much as love as possible, then the fair becomes a love affair in which everything is fair
- When I raise the sword . . . it first comes close to my head and whispers in my ears, "It's a myth that am used by the courageous, actually am used by the ones that fear."
- Wave becomes the Way . . . Path becomes Play . . .
- Only when we drop our ego away . . .
- Great Flyers are those who feel that the wind under their wings is in fact a divine hand, around which they play and stand
- "Real SEEING is when I SEE the SEER, which has being SEEING me forever. The Seer becomes the Scene and the Scene becomes the Seer . . ."
- Any position is mere imposition . . .
- Buddhahood is shunya and shunya does not have sides . . . in infinity nothing is up, nothing is down, nothing is at the front nothing is at the back . . . We cannot avoid the void
- A good instrument is like a strong raju, i.e. solid outside and spacious inside, so that it becomes a flute and resonate the music of life . . . and we are nothing but the present instruments of life, it is up to us how we give birth to the future . . .
- Self-witnessing is not just being aware of self, but being aware of everything around. I become so exclusive that everything becomes inclusive.
- An Angle where ego leaves and love lives makes you an Angel . . .
- Greatest gift I can give to the world is becoming 'a way' instead of being 'away'
- I may not have leaves but love never leaves me . . .
- If you are in sync then you cannot sink
- The one who is present 100% in the present can present the best present
- The real taste of love is when we pass through the last test of life, And it is the woman who cures man with her care, serves him her sacrifice and lives together when everyone else leaves . . .

- Imagination is about Image, i.e. whatever we imagine it will be an image.
- If we want "To Gather" life, we have to live "Together."
- Togetherness or Teamwork begins from within . . . if you can integrate your soul, mind and body, then you can integrate with anybody. If you are divided inside, you will be divided outside . . . .
- We are Blessed with Bliss when we move from 'Become' to 'Be Calm.' Mind craves to 'Become' something, whereas Soul seeks how to 'Be Calm' even amid of Storm . . . .
- Until we have an EXCUSE to FAIL, we cannot USE our greatest strength to SAIL
- DOOR and DOER are made for each other. When the 'O' of Opportunity in DO'O'R is Executed by 'E' it becomes DO'E'R
- GENIUS= Genie in Us. God and Ghost both lurk in us, whom we invoke is up to us.
- I have another paradigm of Empathy . . . . Cannot I put aside/forget my feet and shoes completely? Cannot we feel other's feet (pain) and give him/her the right shoes (solution)? "Treat others the way they want to be treated" and not the way you want to treat them.
- When I surrender to the flow of life, God renders me the glow of life.
- Life is so feminine . . . . the more we define the more we confine . . . feel the love shine . . . love and love is the only sign through which we can destine the divine.
- Solution of any Problem is like a Solution of Chemistry.
- Ego is the solid Solute and Love the super Solvent . . . . In true Love (Solvent) the Ego (Solute) has to dissolve and thus Life becomes a great Solution . . .
- Binding is Blind
- If I can feel the leaf, I cannot rest in the forest
- If we tie the rope of life with hope, then death is a lie. Life is an adventure, so respect its nature. Life will find its own way; do not let your faith run away. Without suffering, the safar (journey) of life is like an ocean without water.
- Unless man does not become Kind, how can we call it as Mankind
- Those who just talk, they call it fate. Those who walk the talk, they call it faith. When we begin to hear faith for fate, the universe opens it gate.
- Solitude is Soul's Attitude

- Flash attracts Flash and Flesh attracts Flesh
- If a blindfold can cause restlessness, imagine the restlessness caused when we blindfold our inner eyes?
- The winds of freedom enables the wings of love to fly
- The beauty of spark lies in the Dark, both embrace each other in the same park.
- Truest learning and sharing is in loving and caring
- Emotion means e-motion. If I promise with my soul then I will not miss the goal.
- Habitat reflects habit. Many have a habit of craving and crying and few have a habit of helping and hugging. Let us develop the habit of love and be the true habitat of life.
- There are so many living beings in my body, then how can I say it is my body alone?
- One who can touch any heart can teach anyone. One who can listen to anyone can learn any lesson.
- The profound is found when you hear in you and around the same soundless sound
- When we read SELF in reverse, we see it as FLES (Flesh). If we think we are flesh, we will miss the inner Flash. We have tried as body; now let us realize the flash, which lurks in everybody.
- When we allow the body to merge, the soul will love to emerge
- The moment you conquer your inner rival, is becomes the moment of self-revival.
- Existence neither loves nor hates, but it is an echo. Be careful of ego because whatever you throw will grow.
- A fallen leaf comes back to the same plant. Let us follow our hearts and work hard, we will get whatever we want.
- Winner = Win + Inner
- It's the focus that brings out the best out of waste and stands like a lotus
- We cannot stop a body by stepping on its shadow, how can we stop a soul by stepping on body? Isn't the body a shadow of soul?
- LIFE stands for Love Inspires Freedom Everywhere
- *Jisne 'aaj' ko jeeta, usne har 'taj' ko jeeta*

With gratitude,
Kiran Kurwade

Relationship is Relay-tionship. Win-Win relationship is like running a relay race where we have to ignite, inspire and integrate each other to win a common goal. We are not here to compete but complete each other.

Unless Man becomes Kind,
How can we call it as Mankind?

by Kiran Kurwade

ABOUT THE AUTHOR

Kiran Kurwade
by choice a Behavioral Coach

Founder of Bright Educational & Social Trust (BEST) aimed at enabling the youth especially the underprivileged class of society to live a great life. Kiran is an **alumnus, IIM Calcutta**. A corporate professional having more than 18 years of work experience in Sales and T&D. Has coached more than 5000 learning aspirants primarily from Corporate World since 2004. Aside India, delivered Training Programs at Middle East.

Kiran's mantra is "Learning & Sharing". In pursuit of great life, he is always in learning mode and derives learning from all possible walks of life be it from small children to spiritual gurus. He likes to study the nature, philosophy, management science etc. He delivers training sessions majorly for corporate world and educational institutes, also regularly uploads certain insights on social networking sites like FB etc. likes making friends across cultures and loves to travel extensively. He believes in Instead of cursing the dark, it is better to enlighten it.

He is a Results Certified Coach, accredited with Intl. Coach Federation (ICF) in 2008. He has done a Post Graduate Program in Social Entrepreneurship Mgmt. from SIES College, Navi Mumbai and is a Science graduate

Connect Kiran at kirankurwade@gmail.com
Twitter : @kirankurwade
Kiran is also a director of iWin—www.iwinindia.org

"Receiving blessings from His Holiness Sri Sri Ravishankar, founder— Art of Living. Also seen with us my friend Mr. Prabhanjan Mahatole, founder— Maxflow Pumps"

Campus to Corporate by Kiran Kurwade

Managerial Effectiveness by Kiran Kurwade